Sam & Co

SAM & Co

The Heroic Search Dogs of the Fells

Angela Locke

SOUVENIR PRESS

First published 1989 by Souvenir Press Ltd,
43 Great Russell Street, London WC1B 3PA
and simultaneously in Canada

ISBN 0 285 62936 0

Photoset, printed and bound in Great Britain by
WBC Ltd, Bristol and Maesteg.

CONTENTS

	Preface	11
1	A Dog with Nine Lives?	17
2	A Different World	31
3	A Careful Sort of Chap	44
4	Casualty on Ravensfell	62
5	'Nowt but a La'al Tiff'	76
6	A Race against Time?	96
7	International Call-Out	116
8	'The Worst Weather for Twenty Years'	134
9	'Loch's Missing'	151
10	Voices of SARDA	167
11	A Strange Indication	186
12	Bivvy Down Brown	194
13	Lockerbie	200
	Epilogue	208

In memory of Alan Thornhill, priest, writer and best of friends, who died just as this book was being completed, and who found in the quiet heroism of those involved in Mountain Rescue an inspiration. I shall never forget him.

Where necessary, names and locations which might unintentionally bear similarities to individual MRT incidents, and thus cause distress to relatives and friends of accident victims, have been changed or removed entirely. This book is intended to provide a broad picture of Search Dog activities, and all characters are fictitious, apart from SARDA handlers themselves, in some cases their families, and the SARDA dogs. With the exception of Loch's work in El Salvador, and the search for her after she was lost in the snow, the call-out on the Annual Course 1988, and the story of Chad, all incidents are similarly to be regarded as having no relation to individuals.

NOTE
Following the publication of *Search Dog*, so many people tried to write or send donations to SARDA that it was decided to include a contact address in this sequel:

Jim Greenwood,
SARDA Treasurer,
Greenstones,
Old Hall Road,
Troutbeck Bridge,
Windermere,
Cumbria.

PREFACE

When I was thirty-seven I fell in love with a dog. Because of this unwary love affair, I am up here now in Cumbria, as I write, with the Westmorland fellside outside my window. It has led me into some awful scrapes, scrambling up icy mountains, falling through into underground streams, abseiling over small precipices, getting mild hypothermia on the rain-soaked Pennines—all in the interests of finding out about Sam.

So I made a friend, and more than a friend, of a slightly odoriferous, hair-shedding, foolish yellow labrador who squirmed and battered his way into my heart. The result was a book—*Search Dog*—which made Sam many more friends, and opened the eyes of thousands of people to the work of the Search and Rescue Dogs. I met wonderful people in SARDA, the Association which trains and monitors the work of dogs and handlers, and in the Mountain Rescue teams of the Lake District and beyond. They became very important to me. Cumbria became important to me. My sister was here already. We knew that one day we wanted to be here, but at Christmas 1987 we made the decision. My husband gave up his job in the City and started his own business up here. I was sort of free (despite two smallish children and a very untidy house and three dogs and three cats of my own!) to write a second book about Sam and many more of the SARDA dogs, and about the work of Mountain Rescue here in the Lake District.

Sam's extended family have become special friends. My admiration for all those I have worked with, and my gratitude, are beyond words. It will embarrass them extremely if I say I feel privileged to have been part of it all for a little while, and that it has been an inspiration.

For the writing of this book, I have so many people to whom I must express my gratitude. Above all, I want to say thank you to John Brown, without whom it would have been impossible even to begin, for his endless, unselfish help at all times. And to his wife Tina, always the calm centre of their house, for her support and valued friendship. And to Dave Riley and his wife Sheila for the stories of Loch and the photographs and cuttings which they so kindly lent me, and for Dave's enormous help in his capacity as SARDA training officer. I have also to thank the other officers of SARDA—in particular Pete Durst, Chairman, Dave Brown, Secretary, and Neville Sharp, Obedience Adviser—for their help and support, and for allowing me to quote from verbal and written comments. Among other SARDA members, I must thank Phil Haigh for giving me such insight into the thoughts and feelings of a SARDA handler, and for his beautifully written piece on the February 1988 search which, with typical kindness and generosity, he has allowed me to use and quote from. Also thanks to 'Kipp' (Ian Brown) and Neil Powell of SARDA Ireland, for marvellous, funny (and sometimes sad) written contributions; Malcolm Grindrod for much information and help; Bill Parr of SARDA Southern Scotland; Jim Coyle, team leader of Cockermouth team; Ken Saxby; Ian Cutler, an ex-handler; David Watt for his marvellous MRT stories; Graham Percival, Brian Wright and the Cleveland SRT for help with the Stokesley training weekend, the Lockerbie search, and for telling me the story of Chad. There are verbal and written contributions, too, from Dominic Atkinson, who has always looked after me so well, and from others who do not wish to be named.

Thank you to Alison Graham, of Gwynne Hart and Associates, who has done much to promote awareness of the work of SARDA through PAL (Pedigree Pet Foods Ltd) sponsorship. She has most generously given me access, through the good offices of PAL, to many photographs which have been invaluable.

There has to be a very special thank you for the RAF, who have given me so much help. In particular 'A' Flight, 202 Squadron RAF Boulmer, with whom I have now flown three times (the last time rather lumpily, thanks to a 44 mph wind!), whom I now know as friends and whose friendship I value most highly. Their dedication and skill in Search and Rescue is a source of great inspiration to many. I have been so very lucky to fly with the crews and to be given such wonderful help with the book. Very special thanks to the Flight Commander of 'A' Flight, Flt Lt John Williamson, to his family for their hospitality, and to all the crews who have shown me such kindness. In that connection I have also to thank RAF Command Public Relations for giving me permission to fly and for arranging all the flights for me, and to Flt Lt Roly Grayson for his generous help in initiating the process; without him I would not even have known where to begin.

Many thanks also to Cumbria Constabulary, to Chief Inspector George McCrone, and to Inspector Miller, who kindly spared so much time in a busy day to show me round Carleton Hall Police Headquarters and the Control Room in particular, and explain the workings of Mountain Rescue co-ordination and how it all fits together. It was most illuminating and helpful in the writing of this book, and I am very grateful. Also many thanks to Bernard Plaskett who, as well as being a trainee dog handler and a member of Penrith team, is with the Ambulance Service in Penrith, for all his help and advice about the workings of the Ambulance service.

Many thanks again to my sister Stephanie Fearn and her husband Paul, John's next-door neighbours, for their help and support from the very start, and to Steph for beginning it all. I hope she doesn't regret it!

I could not complete this list of individuals without mentioning Sophie Kusel, who took so many wonderful photographs for me. I was very lucky to be her teacher for three years. Sophie is profoundly deaf, but not only coped with a six-hour helicopter flight (and loved every minute of it) and scrambled across Harter Fell on a very slippery scree slope to take pictures of the MRT, but has also gained a whole new bunch of friends in Penrith team and at RAF Boulmer. Her photographs are superb, and bear witness to all she has overcome to be the very exceptional person she is today. Also many thanks to Georgia Shorrock who took aerial photographs for me on the Mardale exercise while hanging out of the cockpit on a strop.

I must give a big thank you to Penrith team itself, John Brown's 'home' team, who have given me such support and co-operation since the very beginning, and whose help in setting up photographs and allowing me to take part in their exercises have given me a unique insight into MRT operations. I wish them luck in their fund-raising appeal to build, at last, a Headquarters of their own after years in a damp stone barn. Also to Stewart Hulse, team leader of Langdale/Ambleside team, for all his help and for the use of his excellent book on mountain safety* which has been most valuable in helping my understanding of the medical side of Mountain Rescue.

Thank you, too, to Colin, my understanding husband, who has held the fort for me when I had to go away.

There are many more people I would like to name, but everyone has given so unstintingly of their help and time that it would almost be a book in itself. I do thank you all from the bottom of my heart for your kindness and your humour and for making me feel part of it, and for looking after me so well. The friendships I have made have been the most important thing of all.

*   *   *

---

* Jane Renouf and Stewart Hulse. *First Aid for Walkers and Climbers*, Penguin Books, 1978.

A romantic footnote: Lara Meikle with her father Tony, both members of Penrith team, have been particularly helpful in giving me information about specific team operations they have been involved in and which I have described in the book. Lara was the stretcher casualty on the second December exercise in Mardale, which Penrith kindly set up for me and for the BBC documentary we were helping to make. It was a very rough day, with high winds making our flight over from Boulmer particularly lumpy (I arrived looking rather green). It was hard work for all the crew, and particularly for the winchman Sgt Mike Holman, who had to winch down and secure the casualty high up on Harter Fell, while the wire was doing very unpleasant gyrations of its own. He was hoping to catch a glimpse of Lara, who had been his girlfriend since they had met on an earlier team exercise over at RAF Boulmer. When he eventually touched *terra firma* and made his way over to the cas bag, he found the casualty to be none other than Lara herself, who had insisted on volunteering despite the bad conditions. He hadn't for a moment imagined, when he had swopped duties in order to have a few seconds with her, that he would be winching her up in a gale against a cliff face on a wildly swinging wire. When at last they gained the welcome safety of the aircraft, after long, breathtaking moments—watched from the ground by Lara's father among others—while the wind caught at the stretcher, he was able to give her a certain brand of chocolates he had been keeping for her in his flying suit, which, the advertisement tells us, you have to go through hell and high water to present to your loved one . . .

Now we hear they are getting married in August of this year. Everyone who knows them offers their good wishes to a very special team—with a triumphal arch of Bell stretchers, maybe, outside the church . . . ?

Angela Locke
February 1989

The lake is pure mercury in the moonlight, a solitary Scots Pine silhouetted in silence. You can hear the dogs lapping the water from the fellside stream—it is that quiet. There is only the distant roar of the becks falling down the invisible face of the fell, and the cry of an owl somewhere in the valley. And as always in the fells, the sound of water makes the silence deeper.

There are mountains on every side, shutting us in. The starry Plough rests on one of the highest crags. It is as if the whole valley holds this light in its heart, a breathtakingly beautiful jewel, and its light is bounced back into the sky.

I think of Wordsworth now, and *The Prelude*, but John is talking dogs, shining his torch up onto the sleeping fell, while Sam and Tyan run on down the empty road. I stop for a few moments, by myself. This is my place now. Sam and John and all the friends I have made have shown it to me, and now it will never leave me.

I look up. The stars, the dark, the lake, the towering fellside. It is mystery and infinity. Even on a night like this, how could I ever find my way into those crags? How do they do it, these men and women with their dogs, how do they seek out the injured and the lost, walking alone among the valleys and on the heights? If you were unlucky enough, or foolish enough, this beauty would break you on its fastness, and never even know . . .

The fells are watching. The torch flits across the cragside like a beam in water, making colour. Above the lake, the crags are as impenetrably dark as velvet, but hard. I look up and wonder.

1

A DOG WITH NINE LIVES?

Sam is asleep in the sun, his paws up, legs splayed out, in an attitude of supplication. He has been sleeping like that ever since he was a puppy. He lies like that, too, when he wants his tummy tickled. Then he is only pretending to be asleep, but watching you with half an eye, just in case . . . the truth is, he has never really grown up. He is still galloping about with toys in his mouth, and fighting over sticks with Tyan, and stealing the cat's food. That's Sam.

We are in the courtyard outside the Browns' house. Sam is tied up after a little foray into the village to see one of his friends. Tyan, who never does anything naughty unless Sam starts it, is sitting beside him, amber eyes half-closed, dozing in the sun.

The courtyard is where it all happens. Anna and Pippa sit on the wall and play with their dolls. Matthew parks his bike here. The door is always open and Tina is usually cooking in the huge, high-ceilinged kitchen which is another centre of life. Sam has his corner by the wall where he dreams and dozes. You would think, if you saw him, that his active days were over, and that here he is, an old man put out for air in the sun. But you would be wrong. Sam, at ten years old, is still an active working dog and although John, out of consideration for Sam's increasing stiffness (and, John says, his own increasing age! I think he's joking), chooses the lower fells to search whenever he can, Sam is still ready for the call-outs and can still work for hours out on the fell in all conditions. He's pretty tough, is Sam, and he's had a tough life, although if he could voice an opinion, I doubt if he would change much of it . . .

Sam has been a Search Dog for seven of his ten years. Those years show on him: there are proud scars. For seven years, winter and summer, he has roamed the fells and becks of Lakeland, the high moors and desolate bogs of the Pennines, and far over into the dales of Yorkshire, searching with his handler, John Brown, for walkers and climbers in trouble. For John and Sam are members of a Mountain Rescue Team on the edge of the Lakes, but they are also part of SARDA—the Search and Rescue Dog Association which trains and assesses all potential dogs and may eventually award the coveted title Search Dog to a very special few.

This year will, in all probability, be Sam's last as a Search Dog. He is due for retirement. He grows stiffer every year and those old scars ache after long hours on the fell. John must train another dog to take his place as part of the team. That is where Tyan comes in. But it is hard for them both.

I have grown fond of Tyan who more resembles my own labrador bitch than a dog. He and Sam are so different. Sam is a doggish dog: it has to be said that he doesn't always do as he is told. Tyan, however, is always ready with a lift of his soft eyes to do as he is asked, without fuss. But it was Sam who barrelled his way into my life and inspired me to stop the book I was working on and write my first book about him instead. It is Sam who pushes in, rootling out affection with his insistent head, lying across my lap and crushing me, galloping round with his favourite watering can in his mouth and soaking my feet. Sam is the crazy, madcap dog who is capable, nonetheless, of spending whole nights out on the fell, patiently quartering the ground in blinding snow and rain. He is vividly, intensely real.

I bend down to tickle that foolish fat tummy. One eye opens and Sam regards me sleepily. He doesn't move . . .

'You've had a fair old life, Sam.'

He sneezes violently and wags his tail upside-down along the cobbles.

'. . . Fallen off a crag in a blizzard. Driven a car down the High Street in Anston . . . And yes, there was that strange occasion when you were found fifteen miles away, in the middle of a motorway reservation. That has never been satisfactorily explained . . . I think you must have nine lives, Sam. And then there was that time when you picked up poison in a farmyard. That was a near thing . . .'

John comes charging down the stairs and out of the door, an armful of papers in his hand.

'Sorry to keep you waiting! I knew I had those call-out lists somewhere upstairs.'

Sam, at the sight of his master, gets to his feet and begins to charge at John's legs.

'OK, Sam. I know you haven't had a proper walk but you have just galloped half a mile down to the village and I did have to come and find you . . .'

I get up off the wall.

'Sam and I have been having an—almost—one-sided conversation about his nine lives.'

John shakes his head.

'He's such a scamp. I still daren't take my eyes off him for two seconds or he'll be up to something. He's given us so many frights over the years . . .'

'Like coming off the crag in the blizzard . . . ?'

John makes a face.

'He'll always have that scar over his eye. It severed the nerve, the fall, and he will always have that rakish look . . . it rather suits his personality, I reckon . . .'

I bend down again and scratch his head. Sam, having worked out that no walk is immediately forthcoming, is lying down once more at John's feet, paws in the air, looking pathetic, while Tyan gnaws gently at his back leg, wanting to play.

John squats down on his hunkers.

'You see those tiny puncture marks on his tummy there?'

I lean across and get a lick for my pains. Two small dark holes just on the chest wall . . .

'And that scar there . . .'

I feel along the side of his front leg. Sure enough, there is a ridge . . .

'I don't think I ever told you about how he got those. He almost never got to be a Search Dog. It was right at the beginning, before we even started training. Tina was expecting one of the children . . . now when would it be . . . ?'

'It was Matthew, actually, and it was in that terrible weather . . .'

Tina sticks her head out of the window and grins down at us.

'Lunch won't be long. Can you find the children for me?'

We start off down the path. There are screams coming from the wood, which probably indicates that my two are playing down there with at least some of the Browns. It is holiday time and we have descended on my long-suffering sister for a week, just down the lane next door.

I can feel a story coming on.

'Tell me about it, John.'

'Tina's right, of course. It was Matthew. He was just about due. It had been a terrible winter. We were getting a bit anxious. The roads were blocked. Snowdrifts everywhere. The thought of getting her to hospital in a hurry . . . you never know with a first baby. Anyway, just in that last week, when Tina was getting really close, Sam suddenly started looking very sick . . .'

*   *   *

Tina had noticed the lump that morning, when she came down to make breakfast. Sam was standing there, just staring into space, looking . . . odd. You couldn't put your finger on what was wrong, unless you knew Sam, but he didn't bounce up the way he did usually. He just . . . stood.

'Sam! Are you all right?' She bent over as far as her swollen tummy would allow, stroking the golden head. 'What is it, old lad? Is something wrong?' He snuffled into her hand half-heartedly, giving her a sad little lick. His tongue felt hot. She ran her hand over his flanks. His coat rasped dry under her hand. Had he been like this for long? Had they simply not noticed? He had only recently got over that bout of poisoning when he had picked up something in a farmyard. Perhaps he was just under the weather. There was definitely something wrong. Then she felt the lump. It was right up against the ribs, close in to the chest wall, and it was very big.

She got up laboriously from her half-squatting position, and ran to the bottom of the stairs.

'John! Can you come? There's something wrong with Sam. There's a lump on his chest. I'm worried . . .'

The vet didn't reassure them as much as they had hoped. He thought it was a cyst. Nothing serious. After all, he was a young dog. Young dogs, by and large, didn't get malignant cysts. It would probably go away. In the meantime, he seemed a bit out of condition. They went away with a vitamin and mineral supplement, and some antibiotics, just in case . . .

Tina spent a restless night. John had been out a couple of days before sawing logs and had got wet through. Now he had developed a cold and was coughing badly. In between dreams of having babies, and the very real restless kicking of her unborn child exercising its limbs, was added the dream of Sam, somehow seriously ill. She felt that something was terribly wrong . . .

Very early the next morning she woke with strange pains in her stomach and back. John was in a deep sleep, radiating heat. He was running a fever. The pain came again. Was this it at last, a week before time? If so, she was determined to get some food inside her before the hospital took over . . . She made her way downstairs. It was

December. She would be glad of the warmth of the big wood burning stove in the kitchen.

She switched on the light. Snow had begun to curve its parabola against the windowpane and beyond, in the darkness, she could feel the deep, shuddering cold.

Sam was standing by the range, away from his bed. He was swaying, hardly on his feet. She ran over to him, her hands straying down to the lump on the chest wall. It was bigger: there was no doubt of it. And Sam's chest itself! It seemed to have swelled downwards towards the floor, puffed out, ludicrous, like some strange broody hen. She was suddenly frightened.

Thank God the pains had gone. It must have been the baby resting on a nerve. John was flat out, streaming with sweat. She would have to get the doctor for him if he got any worse. And somehow she must get Sam to the vet. Why did everything have to happen at once?

The vet looked serious this time. Whatever was wrong with Sam was developing fast. He gave the dog an injection. It was a serious chest infection . . . they couldn't do much more, only wait to see if the drugs would work.

'If he doesn't show any improvement within another twenty-four hours, give me a ring . . .'

It was strange, as though the two of them were in some way tied together . . . John was going downhill. What had started as a simple cold was developing rapidly into a bad case of bronchitis. He was coughing constantly, his chest hurting. Tina found herself running up and down stairs between her patients, taking temperatures at one end or the other! John, knowing that Sam was ill, staggered downstairs and had to be threatened back to bed.

'If this doesn't make the baby come quickly, nothing will,' she thought to herself.

By the next morning Sam was worse. She could hardly find the lump any more, the chest wall had swelled so much. Sam no longer even attempted to lie down. He just stood, hour after hour, while they took turns to cuddle him and stroke him, John refusing to go back to bed, relying on the antibiotics he was now being given by the doctor . . .

The vet looked very worried. Sam's chest was by now almost brushing the floor. His temperature was so high they hardly dared to look . . .

Sam watched dully, his mind fighting with sickness a long way away. He had almost forgotten what it was like to bound up and lick for the sheer joy of life. And John was coughing like an old sheep, miserable in his dressing-gown. The vet looked at them both and shook his head.

'There's only one chance left: the veterinary hospital in Glasgow. They might be able to do something for him . . .'

'Glasgow!'

They said it together, and as if to underline their exclamation, a fistful of hail suddenly hurled itself against the windowpane, where already the glass looked like a child's flour and water pasting of snow . . .

'Yes, well, I say that, but it's out of the question. Just look at you both! If your husband goes out in this, Mrs Brown, he'll probably get pneumonia. And if I'm any judge of human gestation, it won't be very long before you're producing a baby! Any day, I would say, especially after all this upset. There's no way you can drive to Glasgow, even supposing you can get through in this weather!'

On Radio Cumbria that morning the announcer had warned that minor roads in some parts of the county were becoming blocked.

'Just tell me how to get there and I'll take him up . . .' John was seized by another wheezing fit.

The vet nodded.

'Well, it's up to you. But don't say I didn't warn you. Can I use your phone?'

'If you go, I'm coming too!' Tina whispered fiercely.

'Don't be daft,' John hissed back. 'You're in no fit state to go anywhere.'

The vet, hanging on the phone, looked across the kitchen

at them. 'Let's see if they have any space first. I'll tell them it's urgent.'

They stood together, numb with misery and apprehension, while he got through to Glasgow. Sam leaned against Tina's leg, grateful for some support. She could feel his terrible, laboured breathing.

'OK.' He put the phone down. 'I'm sorry. The very best they can do is the day after tomorrow. They're jam-packed. It's a bad time of year. I'll give him another shot of antibiotic, and we'll just have to hope.'

They looked at each other and then down at Sam. He didn't even bother to look up, just stood staring into space, his eyes sunk into his head.

'Sam, boy. Sam!' Tina bent down to him with difficulty.

Sam's tail wagged feebly.

'We're taking you to Glasgow, Sam. We'll get you better somehow.'

But by lunchtime it was obvious that Sam was not going to make it. They had made him as comfortable as they could, propping him up in a corner by the warm stove with blankets, but quite suddenly he no longer seemed to know who they were, and that wonderfully expressive tail was still.

'He's sinking,' John said. 'He's just slipping away from us and there isn't a damn thing we can do about it.'

Tina nodded.

'If only we could get him to Glasgow today. He might have a chance. He's a strong dog.'

John leaped up.

'I'm going to phone them myself, and I'll tell them straight that he's dying. He'll never make it if we leave it until tomorrow.'

Tina put her arms round Sam and rested his hot nose on her arm. His eyes had glazed over already. She felt the great shuddering breaths, and swallowed down the tears.

'Don't die, Sam. Just keep on fighting for a few more hours. Just till we can get you to the hospital.'

John got on the phone. There was still no space in the hospital. He launched into an impassioned description of Sam's condition, leaving them in no doubt that if he didn't get there today it would be too late. There was a pause.

'They've gone away to see what they can do,' John said. 'Keep your fingers crossed.' Tina, squatting on the floor stroking Sam's head, closed her eyes and wished fervently.

'Yes. Hello. Well, I really . . . he honestly isn't going to make it. In fact, even now it will be very much touch and go . . . You will? That's fantastic! I can't tell you how grateful we are. We'll get him there just as soon as we can!'

John was galvanised into action. His fever seemed to have been shaken from him. Within a few minutes they were packed and ready to go. John carried Sam out to the car, swathed in his own woolly blanket against the cold, his head on John's shoulder. Tina hovered anxiously behind. Please don't let the baby come now. Please. Just one more day . . .

It was an awful journey, made on silent, almost empty roads. Even with the car heater going full blast it was still very cold in the old car, and Tina was doubly anxious for John and Sam, both of whom were wrapped now in several layers of blankets and coats. And Sam was so terribly still.

It was dark by the time they got there, the short northern days giving so little light. John peered through the windscreen where the snow streamed at them in the headlights, cursing and coughing while he struggled to find his way along the slippery roads . . .

*　　　*　　　*

'I'm afraid he's too sick for us to operate on him tonight, Mr Brown.' The vet was being kind. 'We'll keep him here and do our best, but I have to tell you, we don't hold out much hope for him. He's a very sick dog indeed . . . We'll phone you as soon as we know anything . . . You had best get home while you can. The snow is getting worse by the hour.'

Still half-wrapped in his smelly old blanket, Sam was carried away from them down the corridor. Light shone on a polished floor. There was a squeak of rubber shoes. Tina thought, I may never see Sam again. And there were hot tears on her cheeks which she was too sad to wipe away. They stood together and watched, down the long, long corridor as one of the most precious things in their world was taken away. And right at the end Sam struggled out of his blanket and looked back, his head limp over the nurse's arm, but his eyes holding a mute appeal . . .

*   *   *

It was a terrible journey back. The drifts were building up by now even on the main roads, and snow ploughs were battling to keep a clear way through. John, having made a massive effort, was coughing badly again. The car heater seemed to have packed up: it was never very good at the best of times. They hardly spoke, both remembering Sam looking back at them, as the car ground on along the snow-covered roads. Tina couldn't bring herself to think that Sam would die. They had done their best. They had brought him to the only place where he stood a chance. Now it was down to him—and the skill of the veterinary staff. She unclenched her hands and tried to relax. It was such a long way back and her back hurt, and they were leaving Sam behind.

'They said they would phone,' John shouted above the roar of the engine, reading her thoughts. 'We must just try not to worry. He's in the best place having the best possible care. Let's just get you home safely now.'

Never had she been so glad to see the lights of home. They staggered in, numb with cold. Tina made tea with whisky in it for John, while he stoked up the fire. It was so good to be warm. They sat in the kitchen, too tired to speak. It was very late. Sam's basket lay mutely in the corner. The silence of the house and the emptiness were almost too much to bear. But she was too tired even to cry.

When she woke up the phone was ringing. Suddenly, she wondered where she was. She leaped out of bed, dizzy with sleep, and blundered over to the phone.

'Mrs Brown. . . ? It's the veterinary hospital here.'

Suddenly it all came back to her and she felt cold with apprehension.

'How's Sam? He isn't . . . ?'

'No. He's got through the night somehow. He's a fighter, that dog of yours. We didn't hold out much hope for him, I have to tell you. But he is still very, very sick and if we don't operate this morning I don't think he'll make it through another night. So we'll go ahead, with your permission. We'll phone you again when we have some news. Try not to worry too much. As I said, Sam's a fighter. If any dog can get through it'll be this one . . .'

John was sitting up in bed. He looked better.

'You're both fighters, John.' She sat on the edge of the bed. 'By rights you should have pneumonia by now. They're operating on Sam this morning. I don't think they expected him to get through the night, but somehow he did. That dog has got guts all right!'

John nodded.

'I must say, I really didn't think he had a hope in hell. But I felt we had to try. But I should never have let you come with me. It was irresponsible.'

'You wouldn't have stopped me!' retorted Tina. 'Anyway, thank God we got him there safely and both of us back home without any emergency midwifery. I must say, I was a bit worried when my back started to ache. Still, I couldn't have let you go alone when you were so ill. Let's just hope it works. I just want to see Sam back in his basket again before too long . . .'

John was on the mend but his temperature was still up. She persuaded him to have another day in bed. All morning she worked alone in the big kitchen. Sam's basket, without his woolly blanket and his toy, was a silent reminder in the corner. At intervals she found herself saying fiercely to herself, 'Keep fighting, Sam. You can get through.'

The phone rang twice and each time she jumped and dropped something. She found herself tiptoeing about the kitchen, half-doing jobs and then doing them again. Once she sneaked up to peep at John. He was sleeping peacefully without that awful coughing, and the sight of him obscurely gave her comfort.

It was a bright day, sun shining on snow in the courtyard, the white light spilling into the kitchen. Soon it would be Christmas and by then there might be a baby to share with Sam . . . her thoughts drifted away for a moment. Then, looking down, she saw once again the empty basket and a stab of loneliness hit her suddenly. What if even now Sam didn't come back?

The phone rang again, making her start.

'Mrs Brown?'

A shiver ran down her spine.

'Yes?'

'It's the veterinary hospital here. We've operated on Sam. Drained all the fluid off his chest. He's still unconscious, but he's stable. He seems to have come through it remarkably well. We are going to have to watch him for the next twenty-four hours, but I think now we can be reasonably hopeful.'

'Thank you. Thank you so much . . . for all you have done. We are very grateful.'

'He's a smashing dog. A real fighter. And he didn't have much of a chance. It makes us all feel good if we can pull one out of the hat like that.'

She put the phone down. Tears were running down her cheeks. She opened the back door and stood in the entrance, looking out over the snow, taking deep breaths of the cold, clear air. Maybe, maybe . . . Sam would be home for Christmas. The sunlight was blindingly bright.

*   *   *

A week later John and Tina travelled to Glasgow to pick up Sam. The baby was late by now, but still showed no signs of arriving imminently. If only they had known that the previous week, when every mile back and forth they had been on tenterhooks! But now the roads were clear, and once again Tina was determined not to be left behind.

They waited at the end of that same long corridor, but now the winter sun shone brilliantly through onto the polished floor. Beyond was in deep shadow, but suddenly into the light came a lopsided shape madly scrabbling along on the end of a lead. Sam had seen them, and he was in a hurry. Halfway there he started up his long howling bark of excitement, before he hurled himself at John's legs and snuffled up Tina's skirt in his usual vulgar way, mad with joy. It was the same Sam, without the terrible puffed-up chest, thinner though around the face and shaved comically down one side, where a massive scar ran under his leg.

The veterinary assistant handed over the lead and massaged her hand, making a wry face.

'There isn't too much wrong with his leg muscles!' She laughed. 'He almost had me off my feet just then. And I'm afraid he's been whiling away the time by chewing up his blanket. You can have it back if you like, but it's in ribbons!'

Tina laughed.

'I think he deserves a new one. It'll be his Christmas present.'

Sam, oblivious of his scar, rolled over on his back and sneezed violently. She bent over as far as she dared. Looking down she could see the small punctures where the drain had been inserted and the great scar new and pink against his shaved side. It had been a close call. She tickled his tummy gently, and his tail banged the floor.

'Welcome back, Sam, welcome back,' she whispered. 'Christmas wouldn't be Christmas without you.'

Matthew made his appearance in the world on 28th

December that year. By then Sam had completely recovered and new downy golden hair was growing over the scars. He was ready for a new challenge, and this interesting pink object which cried and squeaked and smelled of milk was a very interesting challenge indeed! But that is another story . . .

2

A DIFFERENT WORLD

It seems a long while ago now since I first met Sam as a young dog. I had wanted to write about him; I was fascinated by it all. Now it was time to discover for myself what it was really like out on the fell . . .

I had thought that as someone who had walked a little in the fells, I would have some idea of how bad it could be up there. I had been engulfed in icy, clammy cloud on a blistering hot day up on Blencathra, and experienced the iciness of the tops in winter. But this wasn't the same at all. This was soaking clag and a Force Six gale. I was totally inadequately dressed, in bright yellow sailing gear, and I would never be allowed to forget!

It was November, and John and Sam were taking part in a weekend exercise. The graded Search Dogs had been brought up here, into a narrow valley; bodies had already gone in. All we had to do was find them.

The weather screamed at us as we got out of the car. I had on so many layers of clothing that I couldn't even bend to do up my boots. I wondered what I had begun. Sam was sitting in the back of the car, whining with excitement, and when John opened the tailgate he leaped out, barking.

John grinned.

'Even without this, he knows he's come up here to work.'

He held up the scarlet Search Dog jacket. Sam went into crackerdog, his tail hitting everything in sight.

'See what I mean? Stand still, Sam, and stop licking me!'

The other owners were parking behind us in the lay-by

or along the side of the fell, by the field gate. It was my first
sight of the other Search Dogs . . . mostly collies, brindled
and black and white. They circled round each other warily,
establishing territorial rights. I thought to myself briefly
how ordinary they looked, these very extraordinary dogs
who saved lives, some with their coats already dark with
rain, wearing a bedraggled look. I was introduced to more
members of the team. Over the years I would come to
know their faces, to be proud to be part of it all. But just at
that moment I was only confused . . . and worried.

We walked out down the track. 'Kipp', one of the
handlers, made me laugh, making me feel at home. I
endured a fair bit of teasing about the yellow 'oilies': it made
me feel better. Malcolm Grindrod, then the training
officer, whose collie, Spin, I had already heard about for his
'finds', explained to me what would happen. There were
bodies hidden all the way up the valley. He would watch
from the valley floor and monitor the dogs' progress. It was
all part of an ongoing training process, which would never
let up until the day the dog retired.

I was offered the chance to stay on the valley floor and
watch Sam work. But I was longing to be up there, even in
the clag, to see for myself exactly what it was all about.
John must have cursed me, although as always he was too
courteous to make me feel in the way.

I had been used to paths, grading gently up the hill. But
John took off directly across the valley towards the large
section of fellside he had been allocated on the western
flank, straight through two swollen streams, and ploughed
across a section of sodden heather and bracken six inches
deep in water. I experienced for the first time, most
certainly not for the last, the horrible sensation of icy
water creeping in over my laces and up my socks.

At the base of the fell I caught him up. I was already
soaked through with perspiration. I had learned a first
lesson in wearing clothes which breathe, and my feet
seemed to weigh a ton. John grinned at me.

'Do you think you can make it up the fell in that lot?'
'Probably not,' I shouted back. 'But I'll have a go.'
'We have to get some height. Then we work downwards with the dog. You can see where the wind is coming from?'

It seemed an unnecessary question as the rain beat horizontally on our faces.

'I have to send Sam into the wind. You know he works on air scent . . . ?'

I nodded.

'Well, if we get well up on the fell we can take it out in sections, as the wind is coming across at an oblique angle from somewhere lower down in the valley.'

I nodded again, too puffed to speak. We had begun to climb and I was already struggling to keep up, my heavy clothes making it hard for me to scramble. I wished fervently for a path, but there was none.

John forged on ahead. I could see Sam bounding up the crag, sometimes disappearing into the mist, then reappearing again, barking impatiently. The rain was coming down my neck, somehow finding its way through my hood, although we had our backs to the wind. I had more than enough to cope with. There were boulders lying everywhere, the sort you had to climb over or get round somehow. They were slippery with wet. I looked up briefly and experienced a moment of panic. John had disappeared! Above me there were a few yards of bracken. I had a pain in my chest. Why on earth had I begun this? Just to write about a dog?

Suddenly Sam was beside me, almost knocking me backwards, rooting at me with his wet muzzle, a pig in an apple orchard. Hurry up, he seemed to say. I want to get started. Then John was there, hauling me up over another endless boulder.

'You've got too much gear on,' he said, stating the obvious. 'Still, if you do get lost we'll be able to see you for miles.'

'Thanks very much. Very funny.' I paused again to get

my breath. 'I must say I feel like the Michelin man. I can hardly bend my knees.'

'It's not so far now. Then we can begin to work downwards with Sam, after we've covered the top of the ridge.'

I turned briefly back to look down the fell. The wind smacked me in the face. I saw to my surprise that we were very far up. Had I really climbed so high?

John was ahead of me again, a dim figure on the ridge. His voice came faintly on the wind.

'Away, Sam. Away, find.'

I put on a spurt, cursing the lethally slippery bracken. One false step and I would be down in the valley. It was pretty steep here. I could hardly see for the driving rain.

Then at last I was up there, with the wind taking my breath away, threatening to knock us both off the ridge. I looked down. The valley was lost in mist. How anyone could see us from down there . . .

'Where's Sam?' I hardly had enough breath to speak.

John pointed. Sam came past me out of the mist, his coat dappled dark and light with rain.

'Away, Sam. Away, find,' John shouted again above the screaming wind, directing Sam with arm movements as he did so.

I was astonished. Suddenly this slightly overweight, lovable labrador, who had been lurching with his peculiar gait through the sodden heather, was transformed. He took off like a rocket. There was no other phrase to describe it. In a few seconds he had disappeared across the fell into the driving mist and rain, finding his way across the broken ground at top speed, making light of the hazards I had struggled over so laboriously.

'You imagine trying to cover ground like this . . . just with a line search!' John bellowed above the wind and rain. 'And in these conditions! It would take a day to eliminate every boulder and lump of crag and gully properly. But Sam can cover it in a couple of hours.'

'Even in this?' A blast of rain almost knocked me off my feet.

'This is no problem for Sam. He's able to use air scent so he works into the wind. He could even scent a body through a stone wall in a blizzard.'

We began to crab our way across. Sam came back and John sent him out once more, diagonally over the upper part of the fell. The wind increased in strength. I couldn't see anything now through the driving rain.

'Away, Sam. Good dog. Away, find!'

What had I let myself in for?

We worked on for an hour, the rain streaming down our faces, high up on the loneliness of the crag. I was chilled after the climb, my clothes damp with sweat, still stumbling along the ridge, but more slowly now, as the ground became more precipitous.

'How long has Sam got to find the body?'

John lifted his arm and sent Sam away again.

'These are graded Search Dogs, don't forget. The bodies are well hidden. We've got a couple of hours.'

I thought of the warm car, and my two ham rolls and the flask of coffee in the rucksack. Another lesson I would learn that first day was never to leave such essentials behind. I would be as vulnerable to hypothermia as anyone.

John stopped for a moment in the shelter of a rocky outcrop.

'You look all in. Better have some coffee and something to eat.'

He unshouldered his rucksack. I was touched by his kindness, not wanting to take his sandwiches, knowing he had a long day ahead. But it would always be the same . . . they would take care of me, protect me, while teasing me to death . . . It was something special I would always remember.

'Go on. Tina's made me plenty. I can't eat them all. And have a swig of coffee.'

I drank down the scalding coffee, glad of the temporary shelter, of the respite from the cold.

Sam came crashing through the bracken, nosing at me. I remembered I had a chocolate bar in my pocket, rather soggy now. We shared it between the three of us. Sam got the biggest bit. For Sam, that moment would enshrine the beginning of our friendship, with a strong element of cupboard love. From now on he would always have a rootle in my pockets if he had a chance. He has an excellent memory.

'If you're coming again, you'd better get some good gear. It can be expensive, but it's worth it.'

It was easier to talk here in the lee of the rock.

'Tina's got a duvet jacket. They cost a fortune to buy. I'm sure she would lend it to you.' That thoughtful kindness again, which I would find everywhere. Tina giving up her jacket, which would stand me in good stead for so long on the fells, until I could afford my own.

Sam had disappeared once again into the driving rain. It was so cold. I had on all these layers, and yet, because they were the wrong sort of clothes, they seemed to be doing more harm than good.

John had put on his rucksack once again. We had had perhaps five minutes' break, but after the coffee I felt alive again. We put our heads into the wind and walked on.

Suddenly, we heard a barking somewhere over to the side of us. John stopped short, listening intently.

'I think he's found the body,' he shouted at me. The barking came again.

'Here, Sam. Good dog.'

Sam was beside us, his tail beating at the bracken.

'Speak, Sam. Speak.'

I had never seen anything like it. Sam put his paws up on John's arm for a second and began to chomp his jaws together like an old man with no teeth.

'Off! Off!' It wasn't exactly a bark, more of a waffle!

'Speak, Sam. Speak! Good dog.'

John was making a huge fuss of him. He began capering round us both, wild with excitement.

'Off! Off!'

It was funny and wonderful and strange all at once. I felt the hairs go up on the back of my neck.

'Show me, Sam. Show me!'

Once again, Sam took off across the fell, John following as fast as the slippery steepness would allow. I followed more slowly. Sam disappeared and reappeared several times, leading John in.

'Show me, Sam! Show me!'

Sam, sure-footed and fast on the hill, was getting impatient.

'Off! Off!'

That extraordinary bark. I wanted to laugh, but there was an odd lump in my throat. John had disappeared, but I could hear the barking ahead of me, faint on the wind. I stumbled crazily over the crag, wanting to be there. A huge outcrop loomed out of the mist, smooth-sided, streaming with rain. The barking was coming from the far side. I struggled round it, hanging onto the stalks of heather, glad that I could no longer see down into the valley, to know how far I could fall.

There, on the far side of the great rock, snug in a sleeping bag inside a blue and red 'bivvy' sack*, was the body— Louise, one of the faithful volunteers.

Sam was enjoying himself.

'Off! Off!'

'Good dog, Sam!'

I stroked the wet head, felt Sam's pink nose on my hand.

'Sam, you were wonderful. But how on earth . . . ?'

I didn't know much about it yet, but it seemed to me that this part of the rock must be protected from the wind, in a sort of 'shadow', so how on earth could Sam pick up the scent?

* A breathable fabric sleeping bag for survival on the mountain.

The 'body' laughed.

'He's pretty bright, is Sam. I heard him working his way round the rock. He must have picked up the scent somehow. He just used his intelligence. I kept quiet, but I knew he'd find me soon enough.'

Sam did another circuit of triumph, banging everyone with his soaking tail.

The body covered her face.

'Steady on, Sam. I've got to stay here for another hour or so while they do another search. I don't want to get any wetter.'

We said goodbye, and John spoke into the radio, telling the training officer down in the valley that Sam had 'found' and the next dog could begin his search.

'Does he always make that wonderful noise, when he's found a body?' We were out in the streaming rain and wind again and I had to shout.

John nodded.

'Only then. It's quite distinctive. You never hear him do it any other time . . . well, almost never.'

Sam was gambolling ahead of us, freed for a moment from his responsibilities, leaving his personal mark on every other rock, chasing imaginary rabbits, unworried by the steepness of the terrain.

It had begun to slope away sharply downwards. We were still in the clag, unable to see anything much. Somehow it was worse going down, and more slippery. I was glad of my walking boots with their good soles. At least I had got that right!

Suddenly, without warning, the mist was swept away: it seemed by a giant arm. We could see right down into the valley, and beyond. I caught my breath. Veils of rain were hanging curtain-like from fell to fell, as though at the beginning of some magnificent operatic drama. The sun lit up the tops and flashed momentarily on the flooded becks. Clouds moved in stately procession across the tops. Blue sky came and went. It was sheer glory.

'I can't believe it. It's so beautiful.'

I stood still, transfixed. The sun shone on us. Suddenly, above us in the clear winter sky, a lark began to sing. Every frond of bracken dripped diamonds. Was this the same world which we had battled through for two hours? It was hard to believe.

'It's a good place to work,' said John. 'Let's see if we can get you down without your breaking a leg!'

Sam came back to us again. I fondled his wet ears. His coat was steaming in the sun. I could smell the wet, doggy smell of him. He gave my hand a lick and bounded off again with his strangely stiff-legged gait.

I looked down into the valley where the river shone.

'I'm going to enjoy writing this book,' I said. 'Even if I have to get used to being teased. And even without all this, it would be worth it just for that daft dog of yours!'

*   *   *

Search Dog eventually became a reality. John, Tina and Sam became my friends. SARDA, and John's team, became an important part of my life. And because of *Search Dog*, Sam acquired many new friends he has never met . . .

Four years have passed since that first outing. We have brought five 'bodies' with us up onto Wan Fell, on a humid June day which threatens thunder. There are two of John Brown's children, Matthew and Anna, with a friend. My nephews have volunteered to 'body' too. With us are Sam and Tyan. It is to be Tyan's first full training session and part of my research for the sequel to *Search Dog*.

It has been raining earlier, and over the gate the path is a sea of mud. The sullen sun has brought out the flies. I have a new rucksack, and I am already hot with too many clothes, used to working in the winter on the fell.

The boys plunge into the mud with cries of glee. A small herd of Friesians cross the field at a trot, and fetch up behind us. I try to look unconcerned as they come close enough for me to smell their grassy breath. I have forgotten to look to see if one might be a bull. They look very large, and menacing.

Halfway across the field a flock of shorn Swaledales, down in the intake fields with their lambs, charge at us, against all the laws of nature. The two dogs both ignore the sheep, and gallop through unconcerned. The cows increase their pace, and the sheep scatter.

We reach the far side of the field, and I climb the gate in indecent haste, after the littlest child has been lifted over. No one else is bothered by the cows, and it is pointed out to me that this is the fastest I have ever been known to climb anything. My nephews tease me unmercifully. I wonder if there is a better way back.

I am here today, on Wan Fell, to compare the two dogs, and their training. They are so very different. So much has changed since those early days. And SARDA has also changed since we began. Then Sam was a young dog, in his prime, and SARDA a young organisation with much still to prove. It is different now.

John is pleased to see that Tyan is perfectly behaved as we cross the field, even when the sheep mill around him. I remember how Sam learned his lesson after being charged by a furious ewe, who was defending her lamb. It was a lesson he has never forgotten. And Tyan will take his cue from Sam, in this as in everything.

We climb on up the path, Sam forging ahead with that peculiar sideways gallop of his. Tyan follows respectfully. I stop, puffed out, and John laughs at me. I am out of practice now.

We come to an open area at the top of the fell, of bracken and scrubby pine. John calls Sam to him, and puts him on the lead. Tyan sits quietly beside him, both dogs panting with the heat. John turns to me.

'I'm going to put the bodies in for Tyan first. Just take the dogs round the other way.'

He walks on through the bracken, with the children

running ahead. He will hide them out across the fell, while the dogs are not looking, deep in the bracken, or up there, behind the stand of pines. Then the dogs must quarter the ground and search them out, using air scent, and working into and across the wind.

After a few moments, when the bodies are well hidden and have been given instructions not to move, John whistles for Tyan, who is off the lead but walking obediently to heel, facing downwind, away from the bodies. He turns and bounds back, his tail wagging eagerly. Sam, still on the lead, almost jerks me off my feet, barking with excitement, ready to begin. But it is Tyan's moment now.

Tyan turns for a second, one paw raised, to look at Sam. He is puzzled, not used to doing it on his own. Sam barks again loudly, in protest, and then Tyan is off.

Tyan is working well. He has been training with John for a year now, learning from Sam. John sends him away in diagonal runs into the wind, so that he covers all the ground in sections. John's voice floats down to us:

'Away, Tyan. Away, find!'

Sam shivers against me and lets out a strangled bark. It is very hard for him. Tyan has picked up the scent on the wind of the first of the bodies and, with a lot of encouragement, he runs in and finds Timothy, my nephew, buried in the bracken. John encourages Tyan back to him.

Now is the crucial moment. Tyan has been so used to having Sam alongside. Now he is on his own. Can he 'speak' to John, telling him that he has found a body on the fell? It may seem superfluous up here in bright sunlight, when we can all see what is going on, but at night, in a white-out, on a snow-covered mountainside, a dog must be able to 'indicate' with absolute clarity that he has made a 'find'. Then there is no question that it will be a matter of life and death.

'Speak, Tyan. Speak!'

Tyan is running backwards and forwards the few yards between the body and his master. Timothy is playing dead.

'Speak, Tyan. Speak. Good dog!'

Sam, who has been watching intently, lets out a shattering fusillade of barks right by my left ear, and Tyan, perhaps picking up the cue, lets out one distinctive 'woof'. John makes a great fuss of him and asks him again:

'Speak, Tyan, speak!'

This time Tyan barks several times and jumps up at John.

'Show me, Tyan. Good dog. Show me!'

Suddenly Tyan is off, leaping the few yards through the bracken, turning to see if John is following. He is getting the idea, and John is pleased. I am having to hang on tight to Sam, who is trying to get free. With a great deal of encouragement, Tyan leads John in to Timothy, and circles round him, barking. Timothy is enjoying himself hugely and doesn't move a muscle until John has said once more:

'Speak, Tyan. Speak!'

John is delighted and 'reinforces' the find with lots of praise, making sure Tyan knows how well he has done.

I think back to the first 'find' I ever saw, when Sam was still young, and I had hardly begun to write about him . . . that moment when I heard Sam 'speak' for the first time, and I realised what a very special and extraordinary creature this Search Dog was.

Suddenly John raises both his arms to signal Sam to come to him. It is his turn. But I am not quick enough at releasing the lead, and suddenly, from my comfortable nest in the heather, I find myself the victim of Sam's enthusiasm, dragged along helplessly. Nothing is going to get between him and his master, not even a ten stone writer (Sam is a strong dog)! There are shouts of laughter. I reprimand Sam, and undo his lead. Briefly, I feel the vibrations of his excitement through the creamy coat. How I love this idiot of a dog. He shoots off like a rocket, crabbing along the path, elbowing Tyan out of the way, charging at the legs of his beloved master. I pick myself up and follow Sam through the bracken, swishing away the flies which are buzzing round us all. It is Tyan's turn to be on the lead. He comes to me quietly and sits by my side, licking my hand.

'Away, Sam. Away, find!'

At John's command, Sam is off! I have heard these words so often and in such different circumstances. Nowadays they are almost superfluous. After all these years and with all they have been through together as a team, they seem to work more on telepathy than anything else.

Sam begins to quarter the ground, working into the wind without any need for John to tell him what to do.

'Away, Sam. Away, find!'

It is an encouragement, a voice in the dark, sometimes the only link . . . a voice in the wilderness of the night.

Sam proceeds to show off, finding Matthew, John's son, and his friend, the last of the 'bodies', with ease even though they have disobeyed instructions and changed hiding places twice. He still has a lot to show us, and Tyan is not allowed to forget.

John shakes his head.

'It's no good training them at the same time. Tyan is really coming on well, but if I let them 'find' together, Tyan picks Sam's brains instead of thinking for himself, and if I put Sam on a lead, you can see how he feels about that! I shall have to start bringing Tyan out on his own. Now he is coming up to his Novice Grade it's getting crucial.'

Sam gives a great sigh, and rolls over on his back. I rub his tummy with my foot, thinking about the day when he will no longer be the one to leap in the car when the call comes. It will be so very, very hard. Since the very beginning, that red Search Dog jacket, the excitement, the middle of the night telephone call, have been everything to him . . .

3

A CAREFUL SORT OF CHAP

For Richard Thomas the day had begun before dawn. He had asked for an early breakfast, and while the dark still lay flatly on the window, hiding the fells beyond the lake, he had dressed hurriedly, shivering in the deep chill of the unheated room. No wonder there had only been a few hardy souls at supper the previous night. Even at a few hundred feet it was cold enough in the depths of winter. Admittedly there was an electric fire in the room, but years of economy while living by himself had meant that he had only switched it on for the very minimum time before going to bed.

It was important, in any case, he told himself, to acclimatise himself pretty quickly. Living in the soft south he had grown too used to being cushioned by central heating and the warm westerly winds. If he was going to fulfil his ambition and retire here, to the place he loved best—find a little cottage maybe, perhaps invest his small savings in a sub-post office—he must get used to the weather. He allowed himself to think about that briefly . . . the dream of retiring. It would be good to do that. Perhaps up here he wouldn't be so lonely. A wave of depression hit him suddenly, out of the blue. Did things ever change? Would it be any different after all, living up here? Would he still be as lonely, as isolated as he had always been? People were always so difficult to get to know. And he knew they felt the same way about him.

He drew a deep breath, thinking of the dining room, and

of the lonely supper he had taken the night before, of other laughter coming from the corner table, and other people's jokes, and of trying not to mind. Then he thought about the tablets. As a precaution he had stowed them at the very bottom of his rucksack, under his spare socks. But he had promised himself to be strong, and he would never break his promise, he would never start that again . . .

Mrs Williamson peeped through the kitchen hatch and saw the lone walker sitting there, a little ill-at-ease in the empty dining room. She came out with a smile, carrying a large pot of tea.

'Did you sleep well, Mr Thomas? Weren't too cold?'

He shook his head, not wishing to offend.

'We're having the central heating put in this year,' she went on. 'Then we'll be able to open properly in the winter. Now, would you like the full breakfast?'

She took his order, thinking he looked lonely, giving him her brightest smile, and he, nervous of attention, hitched his glasses on his nose.

'Are you walking today? Anywhere special?'

Diffidently he explained that he was a botanist—only an amateur, of course. His proper work, for the Post Office, that was rather different. But he wanted to make some studies close to the tree line. He was preparing a paper, just a small contribution to the Society.

'Not too many flowers about at this time of year. What a shame!' She shook her head.

He smiled back at her, suddenly lit up by enthusiasm. She thought what a nice face he had.

'I wanted to come up at this time of year,' he explained. 'My special interest is in shrubs . . . their survival in winter . . . I saved up my holiday. One day I shall come up here to retire. I might start looking for a place . . .'

She thought of the toast burning, but conscious of his loneliness, was reluctant to leave.

'Just a sec. I'll be back. I'll get your order. You must be in a hurry to get off.'

He sat eating his cereal. People weren't really interested. You could tell. The dining room shone empty under the neon lights.

Mrs Williamson came bustling back with a huge plate filled with black pudding, bacon, two eggs, two sausages, baked beans and fried bread.

'You'll need a good breakfast. Mind, the plate's hot.' She radiated warmth at him and despite his loneliness he smiled back.

'So you're walking today . . . looking for flowers?'

He winced. 'Well, shrub life. I hope to go up onto Crock Fell from this side. The scree is very interesting as a habitat, even in winter. I'll see how far I get. I'll take the car over to the back of the fell . . . The Barrow, isn't it?'

She nodded.

'Well, sign the book before you go,' she said. 'My husband's very particular. There have been quite a few walkers lost in this valley. Specially come wintertime, it can be dangerous. If you don't mind me saying, be careful by yourself.'

He nodded, looking down at his plate.

'I've had a fair bit of experience. I used to walk in the Alps. I've got all the right clothing. And I do know how lethal the weather can be up here. I'll make sure I'm back well before dark . . .'

He looked up, but she was halfway across the room already, a smile on her face for the other guests who were standing in the doorway. He stopped in mid-sentence, feeling foolish. It was always like that. People tried, but they didn't really want you . . . not too near. It seemed suddenly that everyone was watching him. In his agitation his hand slipped a little, spilling tea on the tablecloth . . .

*   *   *

It was the accident with the tea that had done it. He had always been such a tidy person, so particular. He had often thought he would make a bad husband because of that. It had upset his routine, that stain on the tablecloth. He had wanted to apologise to Mrs Williamson, but by then the dining room was filling up, and all she had time for was an absent-minded smile in his direction. Still, she had been kind. And that made it worse.

For no real reason he had found himself driving on down the fellside road, past the point at which he had planned to stop, and as though something had suddenly been released in his mind, he began to think and think, about everything. And when at last he stopped, under the crag, pulling off the road almost blindly onto the short grass by the road, he realised he had gone miles beyond The Barrow. It was then that he remembered he hadn't written in the book.

He ought to go back. There was the juniper to photograph on the crag. He had told Mrs Williamson. But he didn't want to go back. A longing came upon him suddenly to break away from all this. To be free from plans, free from everybody. He rolled down the window. It was high here. Halfway up the pass . . . almost a thousand feet. He could smell the cold. The granite soared above him. It was frightening, being lonely; but up here he wasn't lonely, only alone. He loved the high places. They healed something inside. He felt deep down that he needed to be up there, and if no one ever found him again . . . would it really matter to anyone in the world?

He began to climb. Always his beloved boots, which his father had given him when he was a young man. They gave a spring to his step. He had treasured them and taken care of them like living creatures. It was colder up here than he remembered. The wind buffeted him. He was glad of his warm sweater. He stopped and put on a light windproof anorak. It would be better when he had been moving for a while . . .

He had left the map in the car. He should go back for it. Doing all the wrong things . . . not leaving word, not taking a map. It was all wrong. But he just wanted to be up there. He couldn't go down again, not now. In any case, just here there was a sheep track, clearly defined, which wound up from the road, beside the gully and the beck. And it was clear weather, perfect for walking. There was no danger of losing his way.

He stopped, getting his breath. It was steep now, more of a scramble. Two years on the tablets hadn't helped. If only he had been here, in the fells, he wouldn't have needed that kind of thing. He could have come up here when he had been depressed and everything would have been all right.

He remembered the tablets were in the rucksack. But he wouldn't need them now . . .

He looked down the gully and there, far below, was his car parked on the verge. He was surprised how high he had climbed. The fells were clustered round the road and already he could see more high peaks beyond, shadowy even in the light of late morning, as though they hid their mysteries. He knew he was on the pass, and that here above him, rearing greater with every step, was the huge bulk of Ravensfell. He knew it from the other side. There was a path up to Deer Tarn on the far side of The Barrow. He must have come on another ten miles at least: hard to tell on these twisty roads. Anyway, he knew if he kept going he must surely find a path from this side up to Deer Tarn. First he would stop and have a sandwich and a cup of coffee, and then he would walk on. He knew the way to the summit. It wasn't so difficult, even without a map. He would find his way . . .

But the higher he climbed the more foolish it seemed. To ignore so many of the basic rules—it wasn't like him. It was out of character. He knew that. He ought to go back.

He climbed on. The path had disappeared. He was scrambling now on scree, slippery with cloud damp. But he couldn't admit to himself that he had lost his way.

There seemed very little point in anything any more. After all, who would miss him? Did any of it really matter? His face ached with the cold on one side where the wind blasted him. He thought that perhaps he should stop and finish his sandwiches, have a rest . . . After all, what was driving him on, scrambling on and on up the scree, the rocks tipping under him, nothing but the grey crag above? He no longer knew.

The world had crystallised beneath him, suddenly. He saw how it had been, his whole life. And now, straining upwards, his thigh muscles like lead, feeling the exertion as he pushed on up the scree, there seemed to be nothing left but going on upwards, into the cloud. Not thinking about the loneliness, about all the small humiliations . . . then not thinking any more . . .

Suddenly, with total unexpectedness, his foot turned under him on a loose stone. He felt first a sense of outrage. He was experienced enough, after all. Things like that didn't happen to him. Then, in those split seconds of terror as he began to fall sideways, and the scree, unstable after the rain, began to slip under him, he felt a sudden desperate desire to live after all. Life was very sweet. He didn't want to let it go.

*   *   *

In the new, ultra-modern Control room of Cumbria Police HQ at Carleton Hall a message came in to the Duty Inspector, seated in front of one of a bank of computer screens. It had come in from the local police station down at Ravensgarth.

'Phone call logged at 18.45 hrs. Informant a Mrs Williamson at Crockmore Hotel. Walker overdue. Believed to be in the region of Crock Fell. Sending Police Mobile to investigate.'

At Cumbria Police HQ a log was opened by the Duty Inspector. He reached for the phone to alert the local MRT leader. They would need dogs on a night like this. A hard frost and a forecast of high winds and snow by 20.00 hrs. Outside, as though to echo his thoughts, the first snow spattered on the black windows. Another incident had begun . . .

*   *   *

'He just wasn't the sort of man to forget a thing like that. He was so particular. You could see . . . Everything just so . . . I can't understand it, forgetting to sign the book after I'd asked him specially, too. His boots were beautifully polished. I noticed them straight away. It's funny. And he was so put out when he spilt tea on my tablecloth. He went off in a bit of a tizz. I think it was preying on his mind. You know how it is if someone's a bit finicky. Maybe it upset his routine . . . Anyway, that's how I saw he wasn't in yet, just before I started the dinners. Because I'd have known his boots anywhere. Well, you don't often see boots like that nowadays. Real old-fashioned. But beautifully cared for, if you know what I mean. Then of course, when he wasn't back by six-thirty and it had been dark more than two hours, I thought I'd better get on to you. Walking by himself in this weather. If only he'd signed the book, then we could be sure where he was.'

The policeman shook his head.

'It doesn't follow. You'd be surprised how many people don't stick to their routes. Specially if he's a bit of an enthusiast, if you know what I mean. They get carried away, maybe. Then you don't know where they might end up. But don't worry. We're calling out the Peldale team. They'll probably put in the search dogs. At least we know pretty well where he should be and he's got a car. That's usually easy to find. You said he told you he would be going over the back of The Barrow. What's the time now?' He looked at his watch. 'He'll probably just turn up. Been down the pub, I expect. People don't think. If you can give me a full description it will be a help. What he was wearing, that kind of thing. Did he take much with him?'

She thought for a moment, a vision in her mind of Mr

Thomas in his neat Fair Isle sweater, his room when she went to make the bed, left perfectly tidy, the bed already made, hairbrush at a perfect angle on the dressing table, a sense of order . . . It just didn't fit . . . a neat pattern somehow disturbed.

'He seemed a bit sad . . . depressed. Until we talked about his flowers—shrubs, I mean. He's some kind of amateur botanist. He was a bit fussy, I would guess. Told me exactly what he wanted in his packed lunch: had to be brown bread, low fat spread. A nice man, though.'

She shrugged her shoulders helplessly.

'I can't understand why he didn't sign the book. He's just the sort of man who wouldn't forget. You get some idiots in here, going up the fell in trainers, bringing in beer, everything's a big joke. Sometimes they'll put something stupid in the book, it makes my husband mad! But you don't expect that with someone like Mr Thomas . . .'

'So he had food with him?' The policeman interrupted gently.

'Oh, yes. A good packed lunch. And a hot Thermos . . . And he had quite a big rucksack. He told me he had all the right clothes, was very experienced . . .'

'Would you say he was very depressed?' The policeman interrupted again.

She stopped short in mid-sentence, her mouth open.

'Oh, my God. You don't think . . . ? Oh, no. I wouldn't want to give the wrong idea. No, he wasn't depressed like that . . . He was just lonely, an elderly lonely bachelor, I would say. No, not depressed like that . . . at least I don't think so . . .'

'Well, I wouldn't worry, Mrs Williamson. It shouldn't take too long to find him. You've given us a good description. The dogs are pretty efficient at night, even in this . . .'

He opened the front door of the hotel. In the faint glow of the sidelights the first hesitant flakes of snow were slipping sadly down. He said goodbye and began to swing the car out of the drive, at the same time talking to Control on the radio, and the flakes began to fly faster and faster in the beam, beginning a wild, insistent dance which clotted and whirled in his vision until he too was blinded by it . . .

'Poor bugger,' he muttered to himself, as he struggled to see through the rapidly filling windscreen, 'I hope they find him soon . . .'

'Police Mobile from Control. We are now in contact with Peldale Team leader. He's setting up Search Control at the base of Crock Fell. MRT members and dogs are alerted and on their way. Please make your way down there and report on situation . . .'

*   *   *

'John.' Bill Nicholson's broad Cumbrian voice came at him down the phone. 'Do you fancy a stretch?'

John groaned inwardly. He had just got in from a late meeting at past eleven, dog-tired, his last thought as his head hit the pillow, 'I hope to God there won't be a call-out tonight.'

It was always tempting fate, especially on a night like this when the air fairly cracked with frost, and there were flurries of bitter black snow beyond the window.

'We'll rendezvous at HQ . . .' the voice went on. 'There's a lone walker, some kind of scientist, supposed to have been walking somewhere in the area of Crock Fell, around The Barrow. But the police have just found his car at the bottom of Ravensfell.'

'But that's miles away!'

'You're telling me!' the voice went on grimly. 'Peldale have been out already with dogs but they've found nowt. They're looking for reinforcements now, and they've asked our team to give them a hand. Could you call out the rest of the East Cumbria dogs? We could do with them.'

John was awake by now, the adrenalin pumping. Downstairs he could hear the banging of Sam's tail. He must have heard the phone, and he too would be raring to go. John was a contact point now for the East Cumbria dogs, several of whom were in the team in any case, but quickly he ran down the list of numbers which he kept by the upstairs phone. The team dogs would meet up at HQ, but some not in the same MRT would make their way independently to Peldale HQ, or to the base of the fell.

Tina too was out of bed by now, tying the sash of her dressing-gown.

'I'll make your sandwiches,' she said sleepily.

Hurriedly John pulled on thermal socks and winter gear, glad of the thermal jacket which had seen him through so many icy nights on the fell. His rucksack was already at the bottom of the stairs, packed and waiting. In there would be the emergency bivvy sack—the large plastic sack to provide insulation and water-proofing—and the all-important sleeping bag which might save his life if he were beinghted, or the life of a victim hovering between unconsciousness and death. Tina added the sandwiches and the hot coffee. It was time to go.

'Thanks, love. I'd better be off.'

He called Sam to him and began to strap him into his scarlet Search Dog jacket. Sam didn't need any telling that this was a working trip. He was excited enough already, licking John's face as he struggled with the straps, wriggling about, refusing to stand still.

'Settle down! We aren't there yet!'

In a few minutes they were out of the house in the dark yard, everything silent in the deep, frost-bound country night. Sam was racing round in circles by the car, mad with excitement. It was so cold the lock on the boot had frozen up and John struggled with the icy metal for a few moments. It seemed like hours. Sam had graduated to a long, barking howl, during which time the neighbours must have delivered a few curses of their own. John tried frantically to shut him up while lighting a match to free the lock. All the time the image of the walker, injured, lost, perhaps dead, somewhere out on the raw fell, was in the forefront of his mind. Sam would be invaluable, in these dark, snowy conditions. He must get there quickly.

At last, after what seemed like hours but was probably no more than a few minutes, he managed to get the doors open, and Sam jumped into the back of the estate, onto his special bed. Immediately he settled down, though still shivering occasionally with excitement, and whining to himself. John screeched out of the drive and onto the road, feeling the car slip under him, cautioning himself to go carefully. He had de-iced the windscreen, but there was ice on the inside too and it was hard to see. If only he had a garage . . . his mind strayed away to the beauty of getting into a warm car in the middle of the night, instead of one more shock of getting into an ice box. Sam barked at him from the dark somewhere behind him, bringing his mind back.

'Quiet, Sam. Good dog.' He heard Sam settle down once again onto his bed, reassured.

The heater was beginning to work, but outside it was deathly cold. Too cold almost to snow, just a shudder occasionally flicking down towards the lights. God, that poor bloke up there on the hill. The headlights picked out the shine of the grass, dead white, frozen still, frozen cowpats in the road where Steve's cows had come past a while ago, mud ruts from the tractor. Go carefully on this bend. You're more tired than you think.

He drove as fast as he dared through the maze of little streets around the town. They were shuttered up, dark, turned in on themselves against the cold. He turned down the track between the backs of houses. A cat ran away in front of him, stiff-arched with fright.

The 'barn' which they used as HQ and where they stored the Land-Rovers and equipment for the team, was alive with lights, figures moving about, loading equipment. He parked his car at the side and went in, blinking a little in the glare of the fluorescent light.

'Hello there, John. Sorry to get you up!' Bill's usual dry humour surfaced even now in the dead hours of the night. When you needed it most. 'Come and get the crack.'

Bill was bundled up in his old balaclava and jacket against the freezing night, ready to go. Geoff Hornsby, the team leader, was standing beside him. He nodded to John.

'They're sending in the SARDA dogs first and there are several other teams on stand-by, ready to come out at first light. I'll show you on the map where Peldale have set up Base Control . . .'

*   *   *

John locked his car and, opening the back door of the MRT 'ambulance', told Sam to jump in. He got in beside Ian, whose dog Shep had just been made up to full Search Dog. It would be a roughish ride up once they reached the bottom of the fell, and now the snow was falling fast.

He no longer felt tired. He was keyed up, ready for action. Sam, his head over the back of the seat, was trembling with excitement, getting up and blundering about in the dark as they lumbered up the fell roads. Ian's brindled collie was not one of Sam's deadliest enemies, but nevertheless a few rumbling challenges could be heard above the engine as the vehicle swung on the narrow road, pushing the two dogs together.

'Settle down, Sam. Settle down.'

He found the smooth head once more on the back of the seat, the hard nose rootling at his sleeve. Then the dog lay down again, whining softly. He wanted to get there and begin . . .

*   *   *

'John, would you take that section there, you see that small valley leading up to Deer Tarn? And Ian, would you cover the other side? We've already had dogs in on this side, up

towards The Barrow, in case he went in from there . . .'
They hunched over the bonnet of the Land-Rover, using
their torches, their backs against the driving snow.

'I don't have to tell you it's getting urgent. The weather's
worsening by the minute. At this rate we'll have serious
difficulties by morning.'

The leader of the Peldale team, who was controlling the
search, sounded grim enough. By morning, in this weather
there wouldn't be much hope of anyone being alive . . .

'We've had a print-out from the Police giving details.
One or two things might be worth bearing in mind. He
might have a tent; he was pretty well equipped. That
sounds encouraging. But the owner of the hotel wasn't too
encouraging about his mental state. He could be depressed,
she thinks. And that opens up a whole lot of possibilities. It
might be as well to keep an open mind. He could have
strayed right off the paths and we could have a major task
on our hands, especially in this weather . . .'

As though to emphasise the truth of his words, a squall
hit them from behind, threatening to tear the map from
the Controller's hands.

'We'd better get started,' John said. There was a general
move towards the cars and Land-Rovers. John caught a
glimpse of Penny Melville fighting with her wet weather
jacket in the wind. She had come across from a South
Lakeland MRT with her dog Ben, and was getting ready to
begin. Four dogs had already been deployed in the
immediate area where the car had been found, but they had
drawn a blank. It was now the turn of the other dog
handlers to go on up, higher and higher, into the storm, up
into the high crag, each one alone but for his or her dog.
Working on trust.

*   *   *

'Away, Sam! Away, find!'

It was a long shot, this far up. They had begun together,

Ian and he, but after a few yards of companionable walking
the track had split, and suddenly they were alone. Sam and
John would take the eastern flank, and Ian and Shep would
search the valley side to the west.

Nothing prepared him for it. The sudden total loneliness,
away from lights and human contact. Especially like now,
with the snow slanting down into the beam of his torch and
the cold fastening on him. It wanted him. It felt personal,
but he knew it wasn't. It was just the mountain being itself
in its own place, and he had no right here. It wasn't
malevolent, as some people said. It was just there. It was
your responsibility to cope. And if you couldn't cope, and
you weren't prepared, you sometimes didn't come out of it
at all . . .

His powerful torch lit up the tussocks of old grass, and
bracken, and the lumps of grey rock. Around any of those a
body might lie . . . it could be there for days, and no one
would know. But Sam would know. Working properly,
Sam would give a fourth dimension. He would see round
corners. He would sniff the wind as it sidled round the crag.
He would be John's eyes where eyes alone were not
enough.

They walked on, John used to the feel of the path going
upwards, the map in his head.

'Away, Sam! Away, find.' He felt, unconsciously, the
wind on his cheek. He sent Sam obliquely across the wind,
at the same time shining his torch. It cut the night like
glass, seeming so powerful, but still the boulders hid their
shadows and the fell, surprised by light, shrank into itself.
Only Sam, using the air, moving in his own way, would
seek him out if he was here.

You knew at night, really, about the puny nature of man.
You knew how helpless you were, in your thermal
underwear and with your powerful torch, and even with
your shortwave radio talking down into the valley. You
knew that the mountain tolerated you, that even over you
it had the power of life and death; that however developed

your instincts were, however well you moved upon the mountain, you were no longer an animal, to whom surviving the elements was as natural a struggle as taking a first breath, because you had given up your birthright long ago.

'Away, Sam. Away, find.'

The crosstalk bursts out of the radio for a few seconds . . .

'Control to Dog Ian . . . any luck? Report your position. Over . . .'

'Reading you Strength Five, but fading. Weather worsening. We are close to Deer Tarn, quartering the left side of the path . . . Nothing so far . . . The scree is very wet . . .'

John, feeling the wind shift towards the northern flank of the valley, remembered the great spur of Marker Fell ahead, hiding the tarn. It was surrounded by scree slopes, lethal in these icy conditions, and after the rain of the previous few weeks, dangerously unstable. But he would have to send Sam in. If the walker had lost the path . . . He began to climb, leaving the sheep track he had been following, sending Sam sideways across the wind. Sam scampered off, climbing obliquely to gain height, his scrabbled paws sending down stones. It wasn't good. It wouldn't take much to set it all in motion. Thank God the snow had stopped, but the cold was intense.

'Priority message. Priority message. Dog Ian to Control. I have a clear indication . . . lower slope below Deer Tarn. Am going in now . . .'

John called Sam to him. He came sliding half out of control down the shale. They began to work their way sideways again, across the upper bowl of the valley. This would bring them closer to Ian's territory. Sam ran on ahead, and John heard, half-carried on the wind, the bark of a collie up ahead. Sam took off, eager to investigate. By now the two search areas were converging at the head of the valley. It was steep and slippery, spurs of rock rearing up out of the dark, white now with new snow on one side, shaved bare on the tops.

'Priority message. Control from Dog Ian. Shep has found a body. Pretty sure it fits the description. Unconscious but still alive. Request assistance.'

John saw a torch ahead, a leaping dog shadow-silhouetted in its beam, tugging madly at something in his handler's hand. Shep was being rewarded with his rubber toy. It was the important moment for a dog and would be part of the same routine whether the 'body' was real or not.

'Good dog. Who's a good dog, then?' That indefinable communication between dog and handler. 'Oh, you are a good dog!' Different for every man and woman and every dog.

By now Ian was wrapping the unconscious form in his own spare gear, talking on the radio, trying to give as clear a picture of the injuries as he could, there out on the dark mountainside with the snow buffeting at him and torches and dogs barking. It was never like the manuals, never like the training. You just had to keep your head. Then he and John, aware that the body was twisted awkwardly, the legs buckled under, slid a bivvy sack under the prone shape, cursing in the dark because the slightest movement out of place might mean more injury. But what could you do when life was ebbing away so fast in the cold which, quicker than anything, could be the end?

'He's freezing underneath,' Ian shouted into John's ear. 'He must have been here hours.'

'And wet,' thought John grimly. No insulation from the frozen ground. How long? Body temperature dropping to a critical level.

'Better put one of the dogs in,' John shouted. 'Shep, maybe. He's lighter.'

The dog's body temperature, higher than a human's, might just warm the casualty enough. A blast of snow hit them then, flinging the torch from Ian's hand, only by a miracle not smashing it, but blinding them both. How long had it taken them to get there? How long would it be till the team arrived?

The dog, used to such situations, went into the bag without protest, careful too and gentle, knowing how important it was. And then John and Ian lay, one each side of the casualty, to shield him from the snow and the lethal wind. Sam too settled himself down beside his master. He grunted to himself, nose buried in the frozen bracken. John shared round his last chocolate bar. The man was white and still and very cold.

'How long do you think it'll be?' John asked. The chill of the wind, now that they had stopped moving and the sweat was cold on them, began to creep into their bones.

'It's a long valley. It could take a while. Especially now it's started snowing again.'

'Is there anything else we can do?'

'Nothing but wait. Let's just try to keep him warm. He's not bleeding too much, only from the cut on his head, and that's stopped now. Best just wait and hope.'

They stopped talking, each listening for the sounds of the team on their way up, searching the blank spaces of the night for a flicker of a distant torch.

'They'll send in a helicopter, once the doctor gets here . . .'

The night and the snow clamped down. Only the radio told them that the team was getting nearer, very very slowly.

*　　　*　　　*

There was almost no sound in the Control room at Carleton Hall . . . the occasional muted burr of the telephone, the voice of the Duty Inspector. Over in the old part of the building, in what had once been a country house owned by the Cumbrian aristocracy, police officers were finishing dinner under the fluted ceiling. In a case on the wall the silver of a Border Regiment, loaned to Police HQ when the regiment was absorbed into anonymity, gleamed in the soft light. They had had to promise to return it should the regiment ever, in a more sympathetic future, take up its colours again. It seemed a world away from computers and sophisticated software and scratch pads and call-signs. But it was part of the same job. Officers and men now had to know all about this high-speed, high-tech world, as well as handling people, and emergencies, and telling children the time. It was all part of the job. And the ghosts of that Border Regiment maybe listened in a little . . .

A few steps away, in the new annexe, the duty staff were busy at their keyboards, their eyes fixed on the screens around the room . . .

'They're having some trouble locating relatives, sir. Seems no one knew he was up here. There's a sister down in Redhill. We've sent a mobile round.'

'Mobile to Control. MRT request helicopter as soon as possible. Seriously injured casualty located up on Ravensfell. Casualty on scree slope. MRT will bring down to Sheepsgarth above Raven's Ghyll. Map references as follows . . .'

'Message received. Contacting RAF Pitreavie immedilately. Will request helicopter assistance from RAF Boulmer.'

The Duty Inspector picked up the telephone. It would be another long night.

4

CASUALTY ON RAVENSFELL

Two Sea King helicopters sat outside 'A' Flight 'Ops' at
RAF Boulmer, bathed in brilliant sulphurous light. It had
been raining and the helicopter dispersal was lit to a sheen
of orange against a black sky. Now the wind was getting up,
it wavered the drooping blades of the rotor. When they
were at rest they seemed almost too delicate to fly; too soft,
too pliable to take this giant yellow creature into the
sky . . .

Boulmer is a private place, and the presence of the last
RAF station in England has kept it so. There are no
screaming jets above the runway and only a few quarters in
the village, and the few who frequent the 'FBI', the tiny
Ferry Boat Inn almost on the shoreline, come for the most
part for a quiet drink and not for riotous assembly. Only
the constantly revolving radar dish gives a clue to the *raison
d'être* of the station's isolated location. That, and the huddle
of buildings well away from the main station—the home of
'A' Flight' 202 Squadron.

The seals are in close to the shore for shelter tonight. It is
a wild easterly which has whipped the Boulmer shore all
day, too cold to snow; the black sky reflects in dark white-
capped water, the few fishing boats huddle to themselves
on the sand. It is a savagely beautiful coastline, where few
people come for pleasure, and the redshank and the
screaming tern can still nest in something like peace.They
have grown used to the clattering helicopters rising up
over the flat inland stretch: they seem only like large birds.

They do no harm and are soon gone, and even the seals duck their shining heads under the moored boats for only a few moments before reappearing to bob darkly again beyond the surf . . .

Almost halfway through his twenty-four hour shift, the duty winchman, a Flight Sergeant, was making yet another cup of coffee in the crew room. The television flickered in a corner, almost unnoticed. He wondered if they would get any sleep tonight . . . if there was going to be a 'scramble' it quite often came about this time, when the weather worsened and the dark came down. There was snow on the Pennines and the Cheviots. He had seen it on the six o'clock news, but if he had cared to go upstairs to the weather room he would have seen it all plotted out in meticulous detail, and he had in any case seen the latest bulletin on the board. It didn't look too good. The weather was a life and death factor. It went without saying. You always had to know what it was doing.

It was the prime function of 202 Squadron Helicopter Search and Rescue to be always on call in the event of military aircraft in distress. Whatever happened that would always have to take priority. But there were long spaces of time when they must maintain the 'Flight' at top readiness, fully trained and alert, ready for that military crisis—a crash at sea, a top secret jet ploughing in over the dense forests of the north. Thus they were able to act out an increasingly vital role in civilian Search and Rescue which not only kept them in training but often tested their flying to the most satisfying level.

In real terms it meant that for many civilian casualties the welcome, often life-saving sight of the yellow Sea King helicopter hovering above them and the winchman coming down was something they would remember—usually with gratitude—for the rest of their lives. And quite simply, because they were the kind of men they were, it gave the 'Flight' a high level of satisfaction to be there, on the spot, where they could be saving lives.

But the worst thing was no action at all, the winchman throught to himself. The endless waiting, keyed up. That morning, after the change of shift and the briefing from the outgoing team, they had flown a sortie down to Newcastle to practise 'blind flying'. Each of the two pilots' eyes were shielded in turn and they were only able to fly on instruments. It was a necessary exercise. If the weather was rough at Boulmer they would have to come in to Newcastle at night, maybe with a casualty on board, guided in by the radar pulses and the glowing bank of instruments.

The winchman had been glad of the diversion—from the endless American soaps on the TV in the corner, from the 'burr' of the telephone which wasn't a call-out. They were 'on alert' all the time. For twenty-four hours they would live with the sound of the telephone in the background, the adrenalin beginning to race, fifteen minutes to get airborne, often achieved in much less time, your brain sorting it out, then it turned out to be nothing but a cautionary call from the Caostguard . . . that was the way it was. Being there was a necessary part of the job. Tiring in its own way, because you wanted to be out there, using your skills.

He brought coffees over to the table, settling down in the corner to read yet again the medical manual which was his bible. It was that thick. He needed to know it well enough to remember every detail when he was down there, below the winch, on the heaving deck of a ship, or on the mountainside, when artificial respiration might in seconds save a life, when the wrong decision about a lift would kill or maim. There was no room for mistakes.

The other members of the team were sprawled out in the chairs, half-watching a game show and chatting desultorily. It had been the winchman's turn to make the coffee this time. There was the captain, a Flight Lieutenant, and the co-pilot, and in the corner seat writing a letter, the Winch Operator/Radar Operator who held a rare rank in the RAF, Master Air Electronics Operator. He was a veteran of

Helicopter SAR. His job and the winchman's were inter-
changeable: they both had to be able to operate the winch
and be winchman in turn.

The word 'team' was a vital one and it set this particular
bunch of people apart in military terms. In some ways they
were very much on active service, in the 'field', and
different rules applied. SAR Helicopter work was highly
specalised, a fact reflected in the unusual ranks which the
winchman and winch operator held. The team worked on
first-name terms, and there was a special relationship
which defied the usual structures. The differences in rank
might be there but they would be kept in the background.
The Flight Commander would take his turn making the
coffee (and washing up!). And the extraordinary skills
which they might be called upon to use at any time were
the skills of an incredibly close-knit team who relied upon
each other utterly.

Meantime, the duty winchman was enduring the usual
grumbles about the coffee, which he affected to ignore.
The last contestant in the TV show had got to the final
round and was being guided to centre stage by a lasciviously
grinning host. He tried to concentrate on details of ejection
injuries from military aircraft . . . so familiar he was afraid
of forgetting. It was always the same.

In the background he heard the telephone ring in the
'ops' room which, with its huge plate-glass windows,
overlooked the flight pan. He was aware of a sudden drop
in talk, a heightened awareness for a few seconds. The
aircraftsman who was on duty poked his head round the
door.

'Pitreavie on the phone. There's a job for you. Lake
District call-out. Serious injury in the fells . . .'

'Let's go.' The pilot was already halfway out of the door.
They raced to grab their gear from the locker, coffees left
to cool on the table. The pilot would be first out to the
aircraft, starting the engines to warm her up, and to do the
pre-flight checks. The ground crew too were already

halfway across helicopter dispersal, preparing to take the blanks out of the engine intake. Within a very few minutes they would be on their way.

A few seconds later the co-pilot was being filled in with all the available information about exact locations. He was making notes on his knee pad. The winchman would also have preparations to make. If this had been a sea rescue he would have had to take the yellow immersion suit, but for the fells in winter special cold weather clothing would be needed for working out on the winch. His mind had shifted up several gears and was operating at double speed as he reviewed the necessary drills in his mind.

They clattered out of the door into a blast of icy night air. Fine flakes of snow pricked at the winchman's face as he ran. The noise of the engines blasted at him. He ran in towards the nose of the aircraft, automatically checking that he was in line of sight with the pilot. The ground crew were finishing their checks. He smelt fuel on the wind as he climbed in. The greenish light of the interior seemed bright for a moment. Then they were strapping in, flying helmets on. He felt the roar of the hover through his body and then suddenly they were pulled away by the rotors, the night down there, helicopter dispersal lit up below them with the stand-by helicopter solitary against the bright pan. The sea swung into vision through the 'goldfish' windows, white waves picked out along the beach, then dark sky again with the moon rising and the distant glow of Newcastle on the horizon, and then the blur of snow on the windows . . . it would be a cold night. He thought of the walker, lying critically injured on Ravensfell, life ebbing away in the lethal cold. Would they be there in time? At least they were on their way . . .

Back at the base, the Duty Inspector put down the phone.

I don't know how these blokes do it. Airborne in six and half minutes! When I think how long it takes me to get out of bed in the morning . . . '

*   *   *

John was suddenly aware of lights coming up the valley. Sam was barking. Had he been asleep? They had put an emergency bivvy around the casualty and over Shep, to shield the body from the wind. He looked at his watch: twenty minutes. That wasn't bad. He stood up, feeling the stiffness in his legs. It was so mind-numbingly cold.

He shone his torch down. Ian was examining the casualty. He squinted up into the torchlight, making a face at John, looking worried.

'Can you hear me, Mr Thomas?'

He bent over again, lifting the flap of the bivvy. Shep, still lying close to the injured man, whined softly, hearing his master's voice. But the face stayed slack and still under the torch beam, the breath so light that there was no smoke of condensation on the air.

'You're going to be all right. The rest of the team have arrived. They'll get you to hospital. You'll be warm there.'

It was impossible to say whether the unconscious man could hear, but words of comfort might do something, might halt the dreaded slipping away of life, just long enough . . .

The snow had eased off for the present and there was an eerie stillness, broken only by the sudden scream of the wind as it came in gusts and then, as suddenly, fell away into silence. The moon was up but it gave nothing more than a diffused glow through the torn cloud. No comfort.

The first torch wavered up the fell towards them and John and Ian both shone their torches, obliquely so as not to blind the team, but giving light and direction. Sam barked a welcome and suddenly the night was filled with voices, a smell of hot soup—wonderful out of the dark—as someone uncorked a Thermos; the team's lady doctor, who had joined the team recently, kneeling down, a lamp lit, brief glow of a match against the rockside, the quiet face of the unconscious man, radio talk bursting out; static; the clink of the stretcher being fitted together.

'OK, lads.'

It was Geoff Hornsby, the team leader. 'This is going to be a bit tricky. Helicopter ETA is twenty-seven minutes' time. We have to get down a bit . . . the suggestion is Langbeck Edge. There should be a bit of a path. Yes, I know, there never is. But it's very icy, so go carefully . . . head injuries suspected, so we can't use the Entonox* even if he were conscious. Be very, very careful. We'll use the "casim", OK? In case of back injury. It's pretty certain after that fall. He's been here for hours. We haven't got much time left.'

He came over to the team doctor.

'Can you spare a moment, Cath?' They moved away a little, out of earshot of the body.

'How's his pulse?'

'It'll be touch and go, Geoff. I can hardly find a pulse at all.'

The routine was safe. You knew what you were doing. You practised every week in the barn, and you made jokes, and sometimes people got it wrong, which did matter but not so much, but you never got it wrong on the fell. You mustn't think about a man dying, just here, any minute, but everybody knew that was on the cards. Routine. You could do it with your eyes shut . . .

*   *   *

Torchlight. Dark. The snow flurrying again. Wind whipping the cas bag. Fleecy lining. Lay it out on the stretcher. Shep crawling out of the bivvy sack, tail going, nose up to his beloved master. Did I do all right?

Lift very, very gently.

'It's OK, mate. You'll be warm now. Don't you worry.'

'Strap him into the casim.' A wonderful thing, this rigid plastic shell, designed by a team member. It stopped all movement around the spine . . .

* A pain-killing gas.

Is he still alive? Don't ask. The doctor says 'yes'.

Straps. Red, blue, red, blue. Shine the torch along. Now the mauve straps. Six men. Straps over shoulders.

'Lift now.'

The long, long carry down. John and Ian walking alongside, Sam with his nose pressed to John's side, an occasional shiver running down his back. Tension and cold. John feels it too. Shep is slow and quiet. He knows something, maybe. You don't think like that, it's bad for morale. Someone slips slightly and curses, but voices are muted. The wind hits. Where's the path? John and Ian use their torches, breaking new ground, light beams spinning away down the fell.

Five minutes to go. They reach the flat. Exposed here and the wind tearing at them vengefully. A burst of static. A new voice on the radio. The helicopter is near and can talk direct to the team.

'Team Control from Rescue 131. Give your exact position . . .'

The helicopter will land briefly on the valley bottom, to pick up someone who knows the fells at night better than the pilot can and to pick up an instant briefing. It will save precious moments.

The clatter of the helicopter rotors is funnelled up the valley in a burst of noise. Then the wind gets up again and they are briefly blinded by snow. When visibility returns there is nothing. The helicopter has landed round the bend in the fell, and for a few brief seconds there is silence.

Geoff gets on the radio back to the Control Land-Rover. Because they are not in direct line of sight he has put in a relay immediately below them, but suddenly he is talking directly to the helicopter again as it clatters into view, great searchlights backlighting the sharp crag above Ravensfell.

'. . . We are giving you flares now . . .'

There is a bright explosion and the valley bottom is lit red. Two sheep are seen scampering away.

'We can do without those buggers under the helicopter.'

Smoke goes up. Helmet fastenings are checked. The wild blast of the wind is suddenly nothing to this huge yellow creature hovering above them, threatening to sweep them off the plateau with its downdraught. The noise is an assault on the ears. You can only think numbly with your fingers. The dogs crouch down, Sam wondering if he is to be winched up, and dreading it. It's not his idea of fun. Smoke is fired from the aircraft. The pilot is taking no chances with the wind.

The door is open in greenish light . . .

The winch operator is by the door. The winchman catches hold of the winch and hooks on. The wind snatches at him as the winch operator is talking the pilot down. This Sea King over land must be flown continuously by the pilot; on such precipitous ground it requires all his skills. There is always a danger of being blown into the cliff face, which is too near for comfort, a grey crag ahead of the searchlights like an elephant's backside. The wind, pulled down off the crag, could knock them off balance, any time, send them crashing onto the valley floor or sideways into the crag. Just a touch of those rotor blades on the granite face would be enough. It has happened before.

The winchman launches out into the blackness. The wind is angry and throws snow at him, determined to claim something back at last. His legs are spreadeagled to stop that fatal spin beginning. Down towards the pocket handkerchief of light blurred by snow. It is always a long way down.

Above him, the winch operator is talking to the pilot, guiding the helicopter and operating the winch. It is good to have someone up there you can trust absolutely . . .

Cath is kneeling by the casualty, feeling for that pulse. She makes a face, then finds something in the neck, hard up against the jaw. He is still alive—just.

For the winchman coming down there is only this tiny square below, lit by all the team torches and the searchlights whispered by smoke. The winch wire whips out in the wind and for a second he is a rag doll, blown helplessly across the face of the crag. Snow hits him in the face. He loses sight, momentarily, of the lights below. Then the world steadies down again and he recovers his bearings, and suddenly he is down, the wire touching first, taking the static to earth. He unclips, hands wanting to help, steadying him. The winch disappears up into the dark. The helicopter, seeming to turn its belly upwards, falls away. The pilot will stand off some distance from the mountain until he calls.

Even with the wind still blowing, it is curiously quiet. They no longer have to shout. Torches shine down on the casualty while the winchman checks that all is well. There is still a pulse. There is still hope. He secures the strop and sends a message out into the dark.

'O.K., Skip. Ready to winch up . . .'

The muted throb of the helicopter fills the valley again, flaring into impossible noise. The searchlights dance above them, bug eyes of some giant creature, blinding the night. The winching wire flies across and somehow, out of the dark, the winchman grabs it as it hits the rock. The downdraught hits them all. Sam, his ears back, presses against his master, almost knocking him off the crag. He is used to it but he doesn't have to like it. Shep barks at the smoke and Ian tells him off.

The winch operator leans out of the cabin door at an impossible angle, beginning to lift. The winchman steadies himself against the stretcher, holding it against the wind. It is a dead weight. The team watch as the small red parcel of humanity swings and climbs. The wind is getting wilder. They are all crouched down looking up, willing everything to be all right. The stretcher seems very small now, framed against the underbelly of the Sea King. The winchman, struggling to keep it steady in the wind, seems smaller still. They are level with the aircraft floor. The winchman is there. Somehow they manoeuvre the stretcher in through the open door, the wind buffeting at them wildly. It is tricky. He is hanging outside in the harness. That is what team work is about. You know you are always in the best hands.

They are inside, out of the wind. The winchman bends over the casualty. The floor tips as they claw their way round the steep crag, the pilot using all his skill to turn the aircraft on a sixpence.

He feels inside the cas bag for a little warmth. There is none. His hand comes away sticky, the blood blackish in the green interior light. There is a very faint pulse. He breaks open a sterile dressing, trying to clean what he can. The MRT has done a good job, but the head wound is very bad. You can't do very much about it except stem the bleeding.

It is cold here, in the tail of the aircraft. He is suddenly very tired. He has sweated a lot on the winch, with effort and concentration, and now the sweat lies coldly against his skin, despite RAF issue thermal underwear. Someone brings him some coffee. He takes a sip, grateful for the quick warmth, and turns back to work again. So little you can do, even with all the training . . . when it is as bad as this.

He feels again for the pulse, in the neck, uncovering the wrist. Then, leaning forward, he feels for the slight breath he hopes might be there, despite everything . . .

'Did I fall?'

It is very faint, a mere whisper he would not have heard above the vibration of the aircraft if he had not been leaning forward. The man's eyes are open.

'Yes, you fell. But it's OK. We're taking you to hospital. Everything will be all right.'

'What's that noise?' Miraculously, the casualty is struggling to sit up, suddenly distressed.

'Why can't I move my legs?'

'You must lie still, Mr Thomas. We're taking care of you . . . you mustn't worry . . .'

'I thought . . .' The voice is suddenly very faint again, eyes beginning to close . . . the winchman has to put his ear right against the man's mouth to hear anything. It is difficult with a helmet on and the aircraft vibration . . .

'I thought . . . no one cared about me. It was very, very

foolish . . . but I didn't mean to fall . . . I didn't want . . .'

The voice is inaudible, a mere breath, then nothing.

'It will be all right now, Mr Thomas . . . We're in a helicopter. Lots of people are caring about you now. We all want you to get better. The mountain rescue team found you and we winched you up . . .'

He is shouting over the noise of the helicopter engines. It doesn't matter what you say so long as it is comforting, gives someone the will to live, stops the casualty from going back into sleep . . .

'Mr Thomas . . . Can you hear me? I want you to squeeze my hand if you can hear me. You must try to keep awake. Just lie still and listen . . . we all want you to get better . . . are you listening, Mr Thomas . . . ?'

There seems to be a slight smile, there in the dim green light, before the slackness returns. Hurriedly he checks the pulse. For a moment he thinks he feels a flicker of movement, but then . . . there is nothing.

It is suddenly a very lonely place, here, by himself, with the winch operator busy in his cubby-hole with the radar and the two pilots locked into the instrument panel in the far darkness of the cockpit. There is no one but him, alone in the dimly lit body of the helicopter with its vibration and its smell of kerosene, to witness the passing of a man he does not know but for whom he has gladly risked his own life— to pluck him away from the angry mountain and the snow.

But there is no time now for reflection. Even as his fingers register the failure of the pulse he is preparing to give artificial respiration. He will keep going until they reach the hospital, until there is no longer any hope, until a doctor is able to pronounce that his efforts have been in vain . . . But for now there is always a little hope . . .

*   *   *

'It was very good of you, Mrs Williamson, to go to so much trouble . . .'

The elderly widow stood in the doorway of the Crockmore Hotel.

'Come in and have a cup of tea . . .'

'He didn't have anyone else, you see. He was a proud man. I often used to ring him up and say, "Why don't you come over, Dick? It's a lovely day and you could be here in a couple of hours." But he would always make some excuse. I was lonely too, you see. I could have done with the company . . .'

'I left your brother's things just as they were . . . there wasn't much . . .'

'What keeps haunting me is . . . did he do it on purpose . . . ? I can't help thinking . . . perhaps I should have done more . . . but he never would live with me . . . he wanted to come up here and live in his blessed Lakes. Stagnant ponds, I call them, no offence meant. Now look what's happened. How could he be such a fool, at his age . . . climbing mountains . . . ?'

'Your brother . . . seemed very happy . . . he was looking forward to a day's walking . . . I'm sure nothing was further from his mind . . . I think he was just a bit distracted . . .'

'Of course now there has to be an inquest . . . it's so embarrassing. It's a good thing our mother didn't live to see this . . . they told me at the police station he was on tablets . . . I never heard of such a thing. Pull yourself together, our mother would have said . . .'

'Sugar, Mrs Parker? As I said, he didn't have very many possessions with him. Just a few photographs wrapped up in a drawer, in his spare underwear . . .'

'Well! Would you look at that! I never knew he'd kept that all those years. When we were kids, we had a holiday here. Dad took us up some big old mountain. It was that cold. I remember crying to come down, but Dickie, now, he loved it. Fancy carrying that old thing around all those years. He couldn't have been more than eight . . . I suppose it must have meant something to him . . . Yes, Mrs Williamson, I'd love another cup. It's all been such a shock. You've no idea . . .'

Richard Thomas, whose life had been without the warmth of friendship . . .

Did he know in the end that a group of men and women had been his companions on a dark fellside, had kept vigil beside him in the bitter cold and, without ever thinking of such a thing, had loved him enough to try, with all their efforts, to save his life?

*   *   *

As they landed in the hospital grounds, the winchman was still bent over the body, trying to breathe life back into it, but to no avail. Now the body, certified dead, would be taken away. There would have to be an inquest for an accidental death. He would have to make a report at his own debriefing. The processes of bureaucracy would take over . . .

He was not a religious man, but he had tried hard and he had failed, and for a fleeting second he, too, was reaching out for comfort in a cold world . . .

Then he pressed the button on the radio . . . It was time to go home . . .

5

NOWT BUT A LA'AL TIFF

It is late on an autumn evening and we are driving through the fells, with Sam fast asleep in the back of the car, on our way to a course by Buttermere.

The fells have that transparent look, a pale wash of water colour, grey on grey against a pink sunset, fading at last like a whisper into the endless sky. It is very quiet and no one feels much like talking. We flick through small grey villages with lights on against the encroaching dark, shut up now against the chill of evening. There a school with old roses climbing against Victorian windows, a new village hall out of place against the grey slate and stone—you wonder how it ever got built at all—a car park empty now of tourists, an ice cream booth shuttered for the winter.

'That car park,' John says suddenly. 'The last time I was here it was a mass of Land-Rovers. One night last winter we had a big search on. It was based in this village. And there, in that school field, that's where the helicopter landed. It must have been like an invasion . . .'

'The residents must have been a bit surprised!'

John laughs.

'It's odd. We got the call-out one evening. And as I said, it was winter, so it had been dark for a while. The village was all shut up, just like this. I don't suppose most of them even knew what was going on. And by first light, we had all disappeared. I was the last to leave and it was unbelievable . . . just an empty car park again, and two marks on the grass where the helicopter had landed . . .'

*   *   *

If you storm out in a temper, after all, you aren't likely to be carrying the proper gear. Most of us have done it. You just need a while to cool off, and when you get back, it's time to make up. The trouble is, with the hills beckoning on your doorstep, and an urgent need for a bit of peace and quiet and balm for a hurt spirit, it is all too easy just to climb and climb . . .

It was a stupid row anyway. Ann Braithwaite could see that. Her husband hated decorating at the best of times. He always said he had enough mucky jobs at work to last him a lifetime. He didn't want to have to do more when he got home. Funny attitude for a self-employed builder, her Mum always said. And if she hadn't made that comment about the curtains not matching he probably wouldn't have blown his top. After all, he was trying his best and he had given up watching the Saturday afternoon match to get it done in time for her mother coming, and it had been a hard week. They were both tired.

She should have been more tactful. But then it wasn't necessary for him to start on about her mother in that rude way, and when she tried to stick up for her to bang out of the house like that, slamming the door so hard the Busy Lizzie fell off the wall. But that was what rows were like. They were both a bit hot-headed. He said she got it from her Mum. When she was a kid Dad used to lock himself in the double privy at the end of the garden behind the rhubarb, just to escape. He would read his paper and wouldn't come out till tea, no matter if you were desperate and banging on the door . . .

Anyway, David was a lazy slummock at times. It made her blood boil. Needing a rocket under him to get going.

She fumed around the kitchen for a while, clearing up. The wall stood there, half painted. Half pink, half cream. It got on her nerves to look at it. He'd be back, when he'd got it out of his system, and give her a chance to say sorry.

She'd give it an hour, then she really would have to get down to the shop before they closed, otherwise there would be nothing for tea tomorrow. And Mum would worry if they didn't put on a good spread. Before you knew where you were she'd be having a dig about how David could have done better if he had a bit of 'go' in him and she didn't know how they could manage on a self-employed wage . . .

The clock on the kitchen wall seemed to be playing up. Every time she looked at it, the hands had hardly moved at all. Then suddenly, when she looked again, it was four o'clock and she had hardly done a thing and the shop would be shut in a minute—early closing on a Saturday—and he still wasn't back. She scribbled a note on the table and left it propped against the cold teapot. They never had got round to having that cup of tea. That was when the row had started. He hadn't taken a key but she could leave the door on the latch. You could still leave your door open half the day and no one would think to take advantage. Thank goodness it was still like that up here, not like down south in the big towns, by all account.

Mrs Gasgarth down at Wharbeck Village Stores was just thinking of closing when Ann got there. It had started to rain and was getting dark by now, and a cold wind was sweeping along the village street, driving the few children who had been sitting on the wall by the church to home and the telly. She remembered with a quick stab of anxiety that it had been a lovely clear afternoon when he had set off and he hadn't even taken a coat—or had he? She hadn't thought to look in the cloaks cupboard to check. But he would be home by the time she got back and she would make a fresh pot and they would make up and have a good laugh.

'Saw your husband setting off in a bit of a hurry this afternoon.' Mrs Gasgarth reached up for a pack of icing sugar. 'I said to Stan, "That's funny, David Braithwaite working on a Saturday afternoon. He usually stays in to watch the match."'

'He went out for a breath of air.' You couldn't keep anything quiet in this village for five minutes, but it wasn't malicious. If you were in trouble they would be the first to help. 'I'm hoping he'll be back by the time I get home,' she went on.

Mrs Gasgarth carefully sliced a cucumber in two.

'Is that about right? Got your mother coming over tomorrow, then? We've got some nice fancies, just came in today. The sort she likes. Yes, as I were saying, the weather's turning right clarty. He were making for Low Bank End. He wouldn't have gone up the fell, though, would he? It were a nice enough day when he set off but it can be a cold spot when the rain and wind get up.'

Ann Braithwaite loaded up her basket.

'Put it in the book, will you, Doris? I had better get back. He'll be half frozen and wanting his tea.'

'He didn't have a coat on, far as I could see.'

Mrs Gasgarth always meant well, but suddenly out of the blue Ann was scared. It made her feel sick. She said her goodbyes as quickly as she could and half ran back down the street, up the little lane at the side of the church, which local people called a lonnon, to the comfortable house he had built for them when they were first married. He hadn't minded then doing the jobs. What had gone wrong? She slammed into the house, shaking the rain from her coat. The teapot was still there, with the note on it. She went to the bottom of the stairs and shouted up.

'David! Are you there?' There was no reply. The kitchen clock stood at twenty-five to five. He had been gone more than two hours. She pulled open the cupboard under the stairs. His coat was still there on the hook. She went back into the kitchen and leaned against the sink. He was a good man. It was a stupid row. She wanted him back. Just to walk in the door and take away this nagging anxiety. Suddenly a fistful of hail hurled itself at the back door, slowly melting in the warmth from the Aga, running down the glass in

streaks. It was that cold out. She would have to light the
fire in the other room . . .

Another ten minutes and she would phone the police . . .
when the clock got to five o'clock. But she would feel such a
fool. What if he had run off, didn't mean to come back? He
had gone out in such a hurry, but had he taken anything?
She hadn't even seen him go. She ran up the stairs,
breathing hard, and switched on the light in the bedroom.
His best trousers were on the bed—he had changed to do the
painting. His wallet was still in the pocket. The suitcase
was under the bed. She hadn't watched him go but it didn't
look as though he had taken anything with him. It would
almost be a relief if he had gone off: at least he would be all
right. She switched out the light and sat for a moment in
the darkness of the room. Outside the hail was flinging
itself at the window and she could dimly see the outline of
the trees in the churchyard swirling against the sky. If
only he were safe. But how could she report him missing,
after only two hours? Yet it was winter. And he had no
coat. And perhaps he had gone up the fell. He used to walk
when he was younger, before she tied him to the
house—the thought came involuntarily. She would be
kinder if he came home. She made a small secret pact with
herself. When he came home she would be different, and
she would tell her mother very firmly not to interfere . . .

She went downstairs again. She would just light the fire,
and in a few moments he would be back, and she would be
glad she hadn't phoned the police . . . Half past five. He
could have gone down the pub. It would still have been
open at half past two, and then perhaps he might have
caught the three o'clock bus to Kendal, and there wasn't
another one back till six so he wouldn't be in till half past.
She ought to wait. You kept reading it in the *Herald*, how
the police got called out and started searching and then the
person was found, warm and dry somewhere, not even
knowing there had been a fuss. The police got cross about
it, she was sure. They might charge her for wasting police

9 The starting point Search and Rescue operation: the Control Room at Carleton Hall Police Headquarters
Photo Angela Locke

10 The Ops Room at 'A' Flight 202 Squadron RAF Boulmer. On the is the Flight Commander Flt Lt John Williamson
Photo Sophie Kusel

11 Air and ground crew beside a Sea King helicopter at RAF Boulmer.
Photo Sophie Kusel

A Sea King helicopter
m RAF Boulmer arrives
l the winchman begins
descent.
to Angela Locke

The stretcher is
ıched up into the
raft . . .
to Angela Locke

. . . and finally John and
eluctant Sam are
ıched to safety.
to Sophie Kusel

3 A Search and Resc
exercise by Penrith tea
Mardale. Sam finds th
'casualty' and 'speaks'
John to guide him in.
Photo Sophie Kusel

4 John radios to the
rescue team . . .
Photo Sophie Kusel

5 . . . who bring a
stretcher to carry the
'casualty' to a lower pa
the fell.
Photo Sophie Kusel

arch Dog Sam, still
g an active working
the age of ten.
ourtesy John Brown

m and trainee dog
out with their
er John Brown.
ourtesy Cumberland News

time, and she would feel such a fool. She opened the front door and, pulling her cardigan round her, stood for a moment in the porch. Hail had peppered the path with white. It was too cold for it to melt, bitter now, and the wind getting up even more; that loose slate he had been meaning to mend banging away over the porch. He was out in this. Without a coat. And he had been away for a long time.

Suddenly she no longer wanted to wait for the Kendal bus. Suddenly she knew with absolute conviction that something was badly wrong. He just wasn't that sort of man. To go off. He had a quick temper, but it was soon over. She was the one to sulk. He would have been back by now. A terrible sense of wasted time washed over her. Her hands were shaking. She stood in the hallway, and lifted the receiver . . . If she could just get through to the reassuring presence of Alec Pattinson down at the police house, it wouldn't be too bad. He would tell her if she was being a fool.

*   *   *

Sergeant Pattinson was having his tea and watching *Jim'll Fix It* when the phone rang. His small son answered it, but after a few seconds of confused conversation to which he was listening with half an ear, he got up with a mouthful of ham and egg pie and went to the phone himself, brushing crumbs off his shirt.

It was Ann Braithwaite from down at Leadale. Nice woman, though with a touch of her mother in her there somewhere, he couldn't help thinking. She sounded upset and nervous. Her husband had gone off for a walk, she said, about half past two, without his coat, and he hadn't got back yet. She was anxious. He was instantly on the alert. David Braithwaite and he had been at school together and they had both pulled Ann Parker's plaits when she sat in the front row. There wasn't much he didn't know about them both. He guessed there had been a bit of a bust-up, but David, now he wasn't a man to stay out after dark like that, frightening his wife. And he wouldn't have gone off. You just knew with some people. It was part of the job. He stood in the hallway, looking out at where the station light over the door, always shining onto the path even when he was supposed to be off duty, illuminated the half window. Rain and hail now. Snow later, the forecast said. He could feel the draught whipping through the letter box. It was a thin wind, all right, no night to be out without a coat. He briefly considered the Kendal bus and the local pub. He would have to check them both but neither seemed likely.

'I'll be right over. Don't worry, we'll find him. Happen he's got himself a la'al bit lost.'

As he spoke he was pulling his jacket off the banister and putting one arm into the sleeve. 'I'll be there in a few minutes. Best put the kettle on.'

Cathy Pattinson stood in the doorway, watching him.

'Have you got to leave your tea, Alec?'

He grimaced, buttoning his jacket with one hand.

'I'd best ring the station but I'll have to get over there quick. Get the details.'

'Who was it, then?'

She was resigned to missed meals and late nights, like any policeman's wife.

'That were Ann Braithwaite, would you believe? David took off this afternoon. Happen they had a bit of a tiff, like. But she didn't say. Anyway, he's out . . . in this . . . with no coat on. I'd best ring in to the station first. Unless he's on the Kendal bus when it gets in' . . . he looked at his watch, '. . . in about twenty minutes. And if he's not in a pub, we've got a major alert on our hands.'

As he made his way the few yards up the lonnon—no point taking the Mobile—the report of a missing person was already being logged at HQ, and the process was beginning.

Within ten minutes Alec Pattinson had taken details

from Ann Braithwaite and was making his way down to
the Dog and Pheasant to check that David had not made his
way there for a bit of sanctuary, although both he and Ann
had agreed it would be totally out of character. There were
folk in this village . . . well, that would be the first place you
would look, but not David Braithwaite . . .

And indeed the only occupant of the sixteenth-century
pub, a popular tourist haunt in summer with walkers off
Wharbeck Fell desperate for a pint to slake their thirst, was
Fred Brownrigg from the Almshouses, eking out his meagre
pension with a half of Guinness by the fire. The landlord
came out from the back, a glass cloth in his hand.

'What can I do fer you, Alec?'

'Seen David Braithwaite by any chance? He's missing,
like. Unless he's on the Kendal bus.'

'David! That's funny. I did see him about kick-off time.
Early afternoon. I thought it were a bit funny, like. He allus
watches big match and there he was, face like thunder,
storming down road . . .'

'Which way?'

'Ay, he were off in direction of fell, though he didn't look
shod fer it. I said to missus, summat's oop. Ay, if he's
missing, they'll be calling out team. I'd better get me clobber
together, and warn Marjorie to teak ower bar . . .'

'I've just to check the Kendal bus but I don't think there's
much chance. I think he's lost, right enough. You should be
getting a call any minute . . .'

As if to echo his words, the phone began to ring in the
corner of the bar, startling Fred Brownrigg momentarily
out of his doze. And at this moment the lumbering sound
of the twice-daily bus from Kendal (one of the few services
not yet axed) could be heard clearly through the window.
Alec Pattinson excused himself and made his way over the
road to where the bus was already stopping to discharge
the last passenger of the day, Madge Winterbottom on the
way home from a visit to her Gran.

By now the headlights were picking up the slow snow

slanting on the wind, and it was shudderingly cold . . .

The tea had gone cold again. Alec Pattinson had told her not to worry and for a few moments the relief of being taken seriously, and not having someone laugh at her fears, was almost enough. But now that she was left alone in the empty house, with only the fire for company, the awfulness of what was happening overwhelmed her and she found herself crying helplessly. He could be anywhere. He could have been run over by a car, lying in a ditch somewhere in the dark, badly injured. He could have been mugged. He could be up Wharbeck Fell, where they used to go when they were courting. He could have fallen off Devil's Beak! The image came suddenly in her mind of the great black crag rearing razor-sharp up into the sky. There was a path up to the summit, but when you got almost to the top you had to shift over on your bottom, hanging on for dear life. They had done it once, screaming with laughter and fear, but from the other side the path plunged four hundred feet down a sheer drop . . .

*   *   *

More phones were ringing in the town and the fellside villages, and the local team were being summoned to HQ ten miles away, or being told to go directly to the car park by Wharbeck village hall. Alec Pattinson, with a couple of local team members, had begun a search of the local lanes and byways around the village, but so far had drawn a blank. A police mobile from Bankside station was patrolling slowly along the main road, but again nothing. It began to look very much like Wharbeck Fell, or the woods around the base.

It was an unusual call-out in that respect. Usually you had at least some indication that the missing person had set foot on a fell, even though you didn't know what might have happened to him afterwards. But this time he could be anywhere—in this pub, in any bed and breakfast, down any lonnon, lying in any ditch within a considerable radius of Wharbeck village. And the worsening weather, coupled with the existing information about the totally inadequate clothing of the lost man and his possible mental state (although Alec had played down these factors to Ann Braithwaite), began to make the situation look serious.

The local team leader, in conjunction with the police, had decided, in view of the circumstances, to call an East Cumbria Search Panel for first light. The local team would begin searching on the fell, bringing in as many local SARDA dogs as possible in the early stages. But notification to team leaders and a request for a helicopter to be on stand-by and if possible to attend the Panel meeting had also gone out from Carleton Hall . . .

John had just got in from work. As so often in the Eden valley, the worst of the weather was being unloaded on top of the Pennines, leaving the lowlands still untouched. Heavy snow cloud lay pillowed on top of Cross Fell. But there was more to come, and Radio Cumbria was reporting worsening weather in the Lakes. As he parked the car on the cobbles the first flurry of hail spat onto the windscreen. It had been a bright day when he set off, sunny and unseasonably warm. He hadn't even taken a coat to work, but now, getting out of the car, an icy wind cut round the corner of the house.

It was always good to push open the front door and go into the huge old kitchen. Tina was cooking something on the stove and there was a scent of jam—blackcurrant or some such—from Tina's new venture. She must have been making up some batches of fruit from the freezer. Tina was now working part-time at the hospital as a dietician, but managed to run the family, make vast quantities of special jams for the health food shops, and reign over the kitchen with its huge range, still with some measure of serenity!

John found himself enveloped in three sticky children, all of whom seemed to have been sampling the jam fairly recently. And Sam, who had been fast asleep in front of the television, came waddling in to say hello, a child's sock in his mouth. Pippa, he noticed, had one bare foot.

'Thank you, Sam!'

He retrieved the soggy remains and made a fuss of the front end of Sam which was barging at his legs. Tyan came prancing in from behind the settee, and a brief territorial dispute broke out about who was going to claim John's attention. (Sam is the boss at all times and Tyan had better toe the line if he wants a peaceful life!)

Tina came down the stairs with an armful of clothes.

'Don't talk to me. I've had a ghastly day. The jam boiled over, and I was late home from work, and one of the dogs chewed up Matthew's school book.'

'Sam! Tyan!'

John looked hard at them both but was met by only the most guileless of expressions in return. Me? Never! Sam, in order to divert the wrath to come, began to barge at Matthew's legs, hoping for a game.

'I had better give you a hand, Tina,' John began, when suddenly the phone in the kitchen burst into life.

'Hang on. I'll just get this . . .'

It was the police.

'Can you notify the East Cumbria dogs, Mr Brown? There's a search on over at Wharbeck. Lad gone missing in very inadequate clothing. Weather's worsening ower there and the forecast is bad. Can you bring over as many SARDA dogs as you can muster? There's a fair bit of ground to cover. We aren't even sure if the missing person is on the fell and we want to deploy dogs as soon as we can . . . The rendezvous will be the village hall car park in Wharbeck. Do you know it? And we're calling a Panel meeting at first light if we haven't had any joy by then . . .'

SARDA had set up a weekend exercise in the South Lakes area only a year or two before, based at the climbing hut on the far flank of Wharbeck Fell. Pretty primitive it was too, he remembered, and a long walk to the pub. But it meant he could recall the area clearly. That might be very important later on.

'OK. I'll be over there as soon as I can.'

Tina didn't need to be told.

'I could have done without this, John. I really could. I was supposed to go and see Mrs Taylor this evening . . .'

John looked doubtful.

'I don't like to drop you in it, love. But it sounds pretty serious. And they need the dogs urgently. I had better phone round double quick.'

Tina made a face.

'I know. It's just the last straw when it comes at a bad time. Still, let's be thankful for small mercies. It could have been the middle of the night, like last time! Keep an eye on the potatoes and I'll make you up some sandwiches while you phone Dave.' David Brown was now the co-ordinator for East Cumbria dogs as well as SARDA secretary. He would contact as many handlers as he could . . .

It was hard on wives—and lovers and husbands—John reflected as he accelerated away down the hill, Sam shifting about excitedly in the back of the car. It was doubly hard when you were left holding the baby . . . and sometimes they had to cancel something they had been looking forward to for months, or Tina, if she could get a babysitter, would have to go on her own. Tina was always marvellous and supportive, but she got fed up, like all the wives. And when the children were grown up, the long-suffering wives ended up bodying in the snow! Whichever way you looked at it, the whole thing had to be a partnership, otherwise you couldn't go on.

The best answer was probably if husband and wife both had dogs, like Alison and Andy Colau over in the Yorkshire Dales, each of whom had graded collies, although now Andy was training up his second dog. How they managed when they had a small son as well, he never knew. It must be a miracle of organisation. Certainly it was good to see them both on the Annual Course with Lewis in his high chair perched between them, and Betty, Alison's mother, there as body and babysitter combined. It was quite a family thing. And then there was Malcolm Grindrod, whose daughters, both grown up now, were experts on the hill and proficient 'bodies'. Now Joy, the elder daughter, was training a collie of her own for SARDA . . .

Sam, resentful at being ignored, whined and put his paws up on the back seat, peering ahead through the windscreen. It was turning into what old Bill Nicholson would call a 'reet clarty neet', or a 'bit of weather' if he was feeling awkward and anyone else was complaining. It was getting thick now, a mixture of rain turning to snow and the odd burst of hail. The villages were shut up against the night, curtains closed firmly, a warm glow of light and firesides. He thought again of Tina with a pang of guilt, after a hard day, having all the children to put to bed. Rescue work was a high, after all. You got the best of the deal. It was exciting and challenging and when you got a call-out, even in the middle of the night, it was still a buzz feeling. It might wear off after hours and hours of night searching in the rain, getting nowhere, but without it, and without the wonderful partnership and the dogs . . . well, he was very lucky to have both worlds, after all.

Sam whined again. John had slowed down to take the bad bend by the farm at Beck End and Sam was getting wound up, thinking they were there already. But it was going to be a longish drive. He would get on the motorway soon, and take that south for a bit. It would cut out the worst of the journey. Dave would have spoken to the other East Cumbria dog handlers, and a few at least would hopefully be on their way now. Most would probably bring their own cars. It could be a long search. John for one had to be back home by lunchtime the following day and would need transport, and Paul, if he was off duty and able to come now, would be on duty down at the police station in the morning. They all had responsibilities to their jobs to worry about.

He drove on in the dark. Eventually Sam, realising this would be a long journey and they weren't just going down to team HQ to pick up the Land-Rover, fell noisily asleep, having crept over onto the back seat and made a nest for himself among John's assorted gear. Lights flicked past on the other carriageway—people going home to warm firesides and a good supper. John realised with a start that he had missed dinner. Hopefully, someone might be around later in the night with hot food. The police often organised the WRVS to provide sustenance during a night search. Their soup and sandwiches could be a life-saver. At least Tina would have fed Sam and Tyan at teatime. He would be fuelled up to go now for hours and hours in the cold and wet, although John had brought dog food in his rucksack and in the back of the car.

He turned off at the motorway junction and within a few yards, the conditions had changed completely. There was snow on the road, where the gritting lorries had not yet reached, and slippery into the bargain. He felt the back slide as he slowed down, still speeding a little after the motorway. There was the steep pass to negotiate before Wharbeck village: it could be a pig in bad weather. Snow was already whitening the road, but once the frost bit tonight, coming back would be no picnic. He drove on slowly, swerving once to avoid a sheep standing absent-mindedly in the middle of the road and another cropping at the whitened grass by the verge. You were glad of motorways to get from A to B, especially in winter, but he wouldn't be without the narrow lanes and the sheep feeling safe enough to stroll about on the crown of the road, although many got killed when motorists drove too fast for the conditions.

The car started to climb. There were more sheep here, Herdwicks, tough and hardy enough to survive this snow. Some would be brought down into the intake fields but some would weather it out on the hill through the Cumbrian winter and still produce their black lambs in the spring.

The headlights lit up the fell ahead, grey with scree. It was going to be a cold night for searching. He reached the top of the pass, and, careful with his brakes on the slippery road, made his way down into the valley. It was another two miles to Wharbeck village but already, looking down from the height of the pass, he could see a collection of moving lights under the fell . . .

*   *   *

Wharbeck team, concentrated into a small area, were on the spot quickly. It had been decided to rendezvous in the village hall, which was closer to the side of the fell where they hoped to find David Braithwaite, and with adequate facilities for a prolonged search if necessary, including a playing field where the helicopter could land.

It was dark and the weather was foul, and they had no idea where the missing man might be, but a decision was made to begin line searching at the base of the fell, leaving the heights free for the Search Dogs. At first light, with reinforcements, the teams would be able to make a full sweep search of the fellside. But at the moment, Search Dogs, with their extra senses, would be the best tool available.

The preliminary line search had already taken place with negative results and the team were regrouping in the village hall for a briefing. The hall was one of those pre-war structures which seemed to be designed to depress and freeze at the same time. Members of the WI often vowed that it was warmer outside than in on a winter's night, despite an antiquated gas fire, which gave off such a strong smell that one had to choose whether to brave the draughts in the far corners of the room or to huddle next to the fire and risk a slow death from poisoning. The caretaker, eager to be helpful, had switched on the fire and the neon lights. The latter added to the feeling of chill in the air and gave a sickly green appearance to the stacked chairs, the formica tables, the faded crimson curtain which covered the alcove and the foundation stone laid by a member of the local aristocracy in 1923 (long since gone on to greater things), as well as to the members of the team, hair plastered with wet, in their orange and blue cold weather gear. The atmosphere was, however, somewhat enlivened by the appearance of two local WRVS ladies who proceeded to set up a table in one corner, switch on the light in the kitchen and set about boiling the giant stainless steel urn which was the usual workhorse of all village functions.

Against this cheerful clatter, Howard Tallentire, the leader of Wharbeck team, assisted by Alec Pattinson, outlined the next moves in the situation to the initial searchers and those who, after a struggle to find babysitters or finish cooking meals, had only just arrived. With the help of a map which he spread on another of the tables, he outlined the projected search pattern and gave out a description of the missing man, although most of the team members knew David Braithwaite well. He had always been an enthusiastic supporter, and he still helped out on fundraising events. In fact it was he who had organised the repainting of Wharbeck HQ, which was in actual fact no more than a stone barn with storage space and light, giving his services free.

Alec was careful not to go into too much detail about the possible reason for the disappearance; after all, this was a small village. But he did hand out a slip of paper with a full description which the ever-efficient secretary of the Wharbeck team had roneoed off for him. By now they were pretty clear that they had a major alert on their hands.

The door opened and John, looked a bit bleary-eyed in the brilliant light, came in to join the meeting.

'I got here as soon as I could,' he apologised. 'The weather seems to be worsening.'

'Actually the forecast is for mist and rain and above normal temperatures!' Howard shook his head. 'That could present a problem with whatever powder snow there might be on the slopes, if it gets too warm. We don't want an avalanche situation on our hands. John, I would like you to take this far western flank of the fell, working up from this footpath here, which leads out from the bottom of the forest walk. It's a popular tourist trail as you probably know. He could have gone that way. He's likely to have stuck to the paths, at least at first, with the footwear he had on.'

'Trainers, according to his wife!' Alec interjected. 'It could be worse.'

The door crashed open again. The spring, which had never worked in living memory, was to become a source of irritation by the early hours, by which time it had been opened and shut at least fifty times. It was Dominic Atkinson from Keswick team, wearing a T-shirt as usual, despite a light covering of snow on his shoulders. He had made good time in his nippy orange sports car. Howard assigned to him the area adjacent to John's. Dominic, with his black labrador Boris, was an experienced handler, but it would be a good idea for them all, with conditions so unpredictable, to work where radio contact would be possible and help not too far away in the event of any problems. They went out of the village hall together. Several people winced as the door fell shut with a massive reverberation. Almost immediately the sound of the cistern flushing in the Gents could be clearly heard. Howard looked round in puzzlement.

'Are we one missing?'

Several members of the Friday night squash team, who were more familiar with the foibles of the village hall, exploded with laughter.

'It's the phantom flusher, boss. It happens every hour on the hour. Started about six months ago. You just have to hope you aren't in the loo at the time!'

Howard raised his eyes to heaven.

'Great! That's all we need. Let's just hope we don't have to bivvy down here for long. No one will get a wink of sleep. Now, as I was saying, a second line search will begin here,

at the car park base, and we'll walk upwards from here, . . .'
he traced a line on the map . . . 'We'll have to leave this
thickly wooded area till morning. Just hope he isn't in there!
The Search Dogs are going to be our major asset until first
light.'

Dominic and John made their way out from the village
hall. Dominic opened up the back of the MG and Boris
leaped out. The dogs circled each other warily, tails stiff.
Then Boris, always eager for a game, lay down on his front
paws, his backside in the air, and 'woofed' at Sam. Sam, too
much an old hand to indulge in frivolities when there was
work to be done, trotted off to the nearest tree, a priggish
expression on his face. John caught up with him and
fastened the scarlet search jacket underneath him and,
reaching into the side pocket of his rucksack, found a
coolight* which he broke and fastened onto Sam's back.

A flurry of very wet snow mixed liberally with rain hit
him in the face. The wind was turning round. It was definitely getting warmer. But there would still be plenty of
snow about, and if it became unstable, it could spell danger
for searchers on the tops. They would have to take care.

They shouldered their rucksacks and set off, confirming
their departure with Wharbeck Control which was already
set up in the team Land-Rover in the car park. It was a short
walk of about half a mile down the road to the fell path
which would lead them up onto Wharbeck Fell. They kept
the dogs on leads. Land-Rovers and other cars kept
arriving, passing them on the road. Phil Haigh and Andy
Colau, over from the Cave Rescue Team in Yorkshire,
stopped beside them to say hello and get the crack, then
David Brown with his collie Tim.

They turned off the road beside an overhanging crag,
and suddenly, as the wind dropped, they were on their own
in the dark silence of the fell, with only the dogs for
company. There was little snow lying, and what there was

* Fluorescent green light.

had been churned to mud by the footprints of the first searchers, who had been some way up here already. But as they began to scramble up the first steep section, the dogs now weaving free circles around them, waiting for orders, the new snow which was falling had begun to obliterate the path.

They reached the point on the map where the initial team search had stopped, where the valley opened out and a line night search would have achieved little. Dominic unfolded the map and they stood together, studying it by the light of John's hand torch.

'You had better send Sam off on this side initially, John, and I'll take the other. We can keep together on the path for a while then I'll branch off down here.' Dominic pointed to the contours on the map. 'The valley looks pretty steep just there. Let's hope he hasn't fallen in that spot. He wouldn't stand much chance in the snow.'

'Trouble is, he could be just off the path anywhere here,' John said.

The dogs were called in. Two pair of red eyes looked at their handlers, waiting for orders.

'Away, Sam. Away, find.' John indicated with his arm to the left, away from the path. 'Good dog. Sam. Find him. Good dog. Away, find.'

Sam shook himself, snorted once or twice, and galloped off up the fellside. John shone his torch. The valley began to steepen at this point, falling away while the path continued to climb up towards the tops. Far below, they could hear the rushing sound of a mountain stream. The wind was blowing erratically across the path, slanting thin snow into the torchlight.

Boris, aware suddenly that work was to begin, was jumping madly around his handler. Dominic grasped him by the collar, and with a brief struggle, fitted him into the special harness which he wore in preference to the scarlet search jacket, feeding his legs through the straps. Next he clipped the coolight on his back, Boris wriggling madly all the while. John meanwhile, had begun ranging Sam ahead of him, down the path.

Dominic knelt in front of his dog.

'Boris! Listen to me!'

Boris came to attention, sitting on his haunches, a tremble of excitement running from nose to tail.

'Listen, are you ready?' The huge black labrador tried to struggle free, but was restrained. Dominic turned him away from the path, pointing him towards the upward slope of the fell.

'Away and find!'

He let go of Boris's collar. The dog sprang away with a wild movement, dashing off into the darkness, drawing green circles of light which wiggled erratically. Suddenly it occurred to him that he wanted more instructions. He came bounding back. Dominic was waiting patiently, and as the dog jumped up at him, he made a great fuss of him.

'Good dog! Good dog! NOW away and find!'

The handler threw out his arm in the direction of the eastern flank and the dog, now much more in control of his excitement, bounded off up the fellside. It was all part of the game. From now on he could work all night, steadily in circles a hundred yards or more from his master, and never falter.

All over the fellside that night, dogs would be sent away from their handlers to quarter the ground. For each handler, and each dog, a different ritual of beginning and going on would be faithfully adhered to. The dog would remember the games of the past. For most the game would be no more serious now than it was in training, although some old hands, like Sam, seemed to sense the difference. No one knew yet what conditions they would face, or if there would be a successful 'find' and whether, at the end of it all, it would be too late for that solitary body out somewhere in the darkness, a body who might be fighting to survive . . .

6

A RACE AGAINST TIME?

It was no longer snowing, but that soft mizzling rain, which the westerly wind had brought, was softening what snow there was to dangerous, unstable slush. For the casualty, if he was sheltering somewhere, the rise in temperature might possibly be a lifesaver, but it was hard going for the handlers, wading through the gullies, where an inch of snow had accumulated into deep drifts with frightening speed. The dogs were floundering, throwing up soft spatterings of the powder snow in their faces, half blinded and sneezing in the clinging stuff. The collies' coats were clogging with snow, but at least here, with their light bodies, they could 'swim' more easily in this almost aquatic environment. For Sam and Boris, both heavy dogs, it was hard work.

There were five dogs on the hill now—Phil Haigh and Andy able to talk to one another on the radio, John and Dominic working on opposite flanks of their particular valley, and Dave Brown on the far side of the fell. Only Dave was able to talk intermittently to the Land Rover relay, which was stationed above them on the pass. The others, in the shadow of the fellside. would be unable to talk for a while, except to each other, until higher up, they were in line of sight.

Wharbeck Fell was tricky. Not only was there the problem of the snow, and now the misty conditions which had come in with the damp drizzle. Because it wasn't a high

Search Dogs on a crag
above Thirlmere. Left to
right: Sam (John Brown),
Ben (David Riley), Tarn
(Chris Francis), Tim
(David Brown).
Photo courtesy of PAL

Search Dog Boris
(Dominic Atkinson) waits
patiently during an
exercise in Ennerdale.
Photo Angela Locke

14 International call-[to] to San Salvador. A collap[sed] building in the city, wh[ere] Loch found a survivor under the rubble.
Photo courtesy David Riley

15 There were rescue[] teams from many count[ries] in San Salvador. The Sw[iss] who originated the ide[a] of using dogs to searc[h] on the mountains, trai[ned] Alsations for this work[]
Photo courtesy David Riley

16 Out of quarantine [at] last! David Riley (left) [and] David Jones of SARD[A] Wales, reunited with L[och] and Meg after six mon[ths'] separation.
Photo courtesy of PAL

Loch returns to work
her native fells. On a
rch and Rescue exercise
guides David Riley to
'casualty'.
o courtesy Syndicated Features

An ecstatic Loch back
h her master after
g lost on the fells in
zard conditions for
r days.
o courtesy Daily Mail

19 Grisedale, scene of Loch's terrible ordeal.
Photo Angela Locke

20 & 21 Loch returns fearlessly to the still snow covered Birkhouse Moor where she had run from her rescuers in blind panic and (below) a week after her ordeal, is watched by an Assessor on the Annual Course. She came through with flying colours.
Photos Angela Locke

fell, there was a fair bit of woodland on the lower slopes, most of it too dense to work at night. Dave Brown on the far side was working his dog along the few forest tracks, but only yards from the path a tangle of old woodland blocked the way. And here, under the trees, it was dark and dank, with no wind. So both man and dog were 'blinded', both deprived of those senses which enabled them to move forward with any confidence.

After blundering about for a while, shining the torch and calling into the still, muggy darkness, Dave was glad when they emerged from the woodland area and he was able to send Tim fast away up the fellside, in a broad sweep up onto the crag. Here, despite the mist, there was a good breeze coming across the hill, and it would be satisfying ground to work.

Tim was responding well, although it was hard to keep track of him through the drizzle and the dark. The beam from Dave's hand torch was reflected back to him in a hazy light, and Tim seemed to come and go like a green fuzzy shadow.

Dave stopped and looked at his map. There was a footpath a little higher up which climbed towards the summit of the fell. It was a bit out the way from the village, but it might be worth a try. He squinted at the map in the dark, wiping its plastic cover with his sleeve. Here, on the far flank of the valley, was the last section of the path leading up to the summit. It led over Devil's Beak, a strange volcanic outcrop which hung razor sharp over the beck below. He remembered walking it with an Outward Bound group years ago. It was aptly named, a treacherous crag in anyone's book. Only last year a couple had been blown off the top. Wharbeck team had found them, not needing to call in search dogs. Hopefully, the missing man would have had more sense than to venture on the path which led along the sharpest ridge, even supposing he had been making for the summit. But in darkness and snow and rain, who could tell?

His feet found the path and, calling Tim to him, he sent him away upwards into the blackness above . . .

*   *   *

Penny Melville and her dog Ben had had a long drive over from Wasdale. The bad weather had not yet reached her valley and she was surprised when suddenly she hit snow coming over the pass into Wharbeck. But as she descended again, the snow began to blur moistly on the windscreen and very soon she found fine rain was taking its place. She drove along the deserted main street, the neon lights in shop windows still lit; a few fairy lights illuminated the sign of The Dog and Pheasant, only a couple of cars midweek in the pub car park; the display left over from Christmas of two snowmen and a Christmas tree still flashed inter-mittently in the window of the confectioners, starring the wet road outside.

Then she turned the corner into the dark again, past two houses standing alone, curtains closed on dimly lit windows, and suddenly the village hall car park was ahead of her. It was alive with lights, including a flashing blue police light catching the tops of cars, the whole place buzzing with activity. The team were just setting off for their second line search on the lower slopes, and several of David Braithwaite's neighbours were returning in their cars from combing the surrounding roads. Although that had been done already by the police, you never knew. She found a parking space for her car, rummaged about for her map and made her way inside.

There was a wonderful aroma of hot soup, which made her realise that she hadn't eaten, having left as soon as she had received the call-out. It was a smell mingled with soaking wet waterproofs, steam from the urn, damp boots, gas and wet dogs. The windows were steamed up. There was a lot of noise, with everyone explaining at once which area they had searched and poring over maps, while trying at the same time to sip scalding tomato soup and eat ham sandwiches. Keith Warwick's huge Alsatian Graf was sitting at his master's feet, looking hopeful, while Keith gestured with a half-eaten sandwich at an area on the map.

Penny made her way over to them, pausing only to pick up a cup of soup from the WRVS lady at the kitchen hatch, who was trying to keep up with demand for soup, sandwiches and tea from the sudden influx of wet, cold searchers baying for hot nourishment.

Howard, the team leader, having somehow assimilated the feedback of information from the various de-briefings, had decided to stand the team down for the night, until the Panel meeting at first light, when everyone would rendezvous for a full search. Now it would be down to the Search Dogs. He had been speaking to Dave Brown via the relay, on the Control radio, and Dave had warned of possible avalanche conditions in the gullies above a thousand feet. The whole snow face was shifting in the warm, wet conditions; it could be very dangerous. Dave was working alone on the far side, although with radio contact relayed to base. It seemed like a good idea to send up a couple more searchers on to the far side.

Penny and Keith were given an area obliquely under Dave's 'wedge' of fell, using a path whereby they could work their way up to him. They would be able to rendezvous with him at the base of Devil's Beak later in the night. Alec Pattinson, who had been liaising with the various elements—Wharbeck team, Search Dogs, Carleton Hall, WRVS—and making sure everything was running smoothly, had also found time to make a couple of visits to Ann Braithwaite, who was sitting at home alone, refusing to go to bed, making endless cups of tea. She had told him about her fears of Devil's Beak and how they had climbed there in their younger days, Alec had passed it on. Now Howard would concentrate some of his resources in that area.

In the minds of some of the more experienced team members, and in Alec's mind too, was the memory of a night ten years ago, when they had brought down a young suicide off the hill. The girl had left a note in her room at home, had climbed at sunset up to Devil's Beak, and jumped off just as darkness fell. Not one of them would ever forget putting that broken body onto the stretcher and the long, slow, sad journey down, to face the distraught parents waiting by the Land-Rover. One way and another, Devil's Beak had sinister memories for them all . . .

As Keith and Penny set off, the Wharbeck team were unpacking sleeping bags ready to crash out for an hour or two in the village hall. It was best to get some rest while they could. At any time a call might come through and they would have to begin the long climb up the fellside to carry a casualty down to a waiting ambulance. Howard was checking through the equipment, going backwards and forwards out of the door to the Land-Rover in the car-park, where the Controller sat stoically waiting for messages, fortified with cups of soup and tea from the kitchen. Howard had also organised another relay to go to the top of Marghyll Fell, a long trek in the Land-Rover up a track to Longbeck Farm. For some while Control had been unable to raise either John and Dominic or Phil and Andy. In view of the conditions another relay was a necessity. Anything could be happening up there . . .

*   *   *

Aaaaaaaah! a scream rent the silence of the night. Andy Colau had been working his collie Corrie through the deep mist which had now settled over the fellside. He had just paused for a few seconds to orientate himself with map, compass and torch precariously juggled in cold hands, while he balanced himself on a slippery patch of snow-covered scree. It was an exercise in co-ordination at the best of times, requiring full concentration, but the sudden sound was so unexpected that he dropped the torch in the darkness and it went out. Corrie came bounding back, ears pricked, fur glowing ghostly green where the moisture-laden air had settled on her coat. He found the torch and shone it ahead. The radio crackled, to be followed immediately by a burst of swearing.

'Get over here, will you, Andy. I could do with some help.' It was Phil's voice. Fortunately they were not far apart at this point, having been checking map references only recently on the radio. Andy climbed down into the small gully and up the far side. He could see Phil's light glowing against the snow.

'Keep away from that wall! And keep the dog away!' The radio crackled into life again as he approached. He pushed on up through the clogging bracken, legs aching with the effort. The wall loomed in the torchlight. He called Corrie to him, close so that she pressed against his knee, trembling still with the effort of scrabbling through the snow.

Phil was sitting against the base of the stone wall, where it snaked high up onto the fellside.

'It's a bloody cattle fence, would you believe!' Phil shouted across. 'Just look at that!'

He shone his torch upwards, onto the wall behind. Three strands of innocuous-looking wire were stretched along the top.

'No indication that it's an electric fence. Gave me a helluva thump! It almost knocked me out. I tried to climb it in the dark. It threw Tosh back. She gave a terrific yowl. So did I, I can tell you. Now I can't find her anywhere.'

'Are you OK, Phil?'

Phil scrambled to his feet.

'I feel a bit shaken, and my skin's tingling . . . as though I'd got a dose of sunburn. What worries me is, if it was that bad for me, what will it have been like for Tosh? She's only a little dog.'

Andy shone his torch up the fellside, through the snow-covered boulders. A line of paw prints led upwards through the whiteness, away from the wall.

'She'll have run off, frightened out of her wits, I shouldn't wonder,' said Phil. 'Tosh! Here, Tosh. Come on!'

Suddenly, a black and white collie appeared in the torchlight, and came gingerly down the fell towards them. She was whining softly and obviously upset.

'Poor bloody dog!' Phil exploded. 'She's lucky to be alive! If I could get hold of that farmer. There's a terrific voltage going through that thing.'

He squatted down. 'Here, Tosh. It's all right now. Come on, then!'

The dog limped forwards slowly, until she was sitting at her master's feet, the coolight glowing still on her back, illuminating the dark coat.

'She must have been thrown back into a snowdrift.' Phil ran his hands over her, feeling for broken bones. 'If she took it on her nose, she won't be much good for the rest of the night. I ought to get her back down.'

The collie was trembling under his hand.

'You go on, Andy, and I'll just keep her with me for a bit. If she carries on like this, we'll have to call it a day.'

Andy shook his head.

'It's a bit daft to go on in any case, Phil. You should stop while you're ahead. You're both lucky not to have been badly burned.'

Phil shook his head.

'I'd like to go on for a bit. If we stop now she won't get her confidence back.'

They started to walk together alongside the wall. Every few yards one of them shone their torch upwards, but the lines of the electric fence stretched on remorselessly up the fell.

'It cuts right across our area,' said Phil gloomily. 'How the hell are we going to get over?'

But as he spoke, ahead of them in the gloom they could see that the wall broke into two branches, running right and left. The wires bent round to the right with a set of rusty transformers.

'I wish I'd seen those before. This fence is not even marked on the map,' said Phil. 'And it's pretty high up for the field edge. What breed do they have here? Something crossed with a mountain goat and a yak?'

As if to echo his words, a reproachful shaggy head, crowned by a pair of enormous horns, appeared in the torchlight on the far side of the wall, a discreet distance from the electric fence.

'Crikey!' said Phil. 'That accounts for it. I don't know which is worse, meeting one of those roaming the fell, or getting an electric shock.'

'We'll just have to cover this area to the left and hope the missing bloke isn't in that particular field. I can't imagine he would be, but we'll have to tell Howard it hasn't been covered.'

Tosh was pushing at Phil's hand with a cold, wet nose. She had stopped trembling and was eager to get on. They clambered with some caution over the left-hand branch of the wall, which was hopefully cattle and voltage free. Here, now, was the open fell. They had left the intake fields behind and would be able to work with only natural obstructions to impede their progress. That, in these conditions, was bad enough.

'I think we can both go on for a bit. You take this side, Andy, and I'll go on up here.'

'Just take it steady, Phil,' warned Andy. 'And keep in radio contact.'

Tosh, sent away on up the fell, took off with every appearance of joy. Phil paused to reflect on the incredible toughness of the average Search Dog, before the slippery and unstable snow claimed all his attention and he walked on in the dark . . .

*   *   *

There were now eight Search Dogs quartering the fellside above the village. Dave Riley, a police sergeant in the South Lakes, had been almost at the end of his shift when the call-out came through. It was a quiet night, with not much going on, so he had been able to get away fairly quickly, go home and pick up his dog and all his gear. He had made his way up to Wharbeck fell, talking to team Control on his radio. He was given instructions to work his way upwards to Devil's Beak from the road under Marghyll Fell, parking his car on the road south, and from then on to talk to the relay up at Marghyll Fell instead of Control.

Loch, his small-boned black and white collie, a great family pet and special friend of his daughter Charlotte, was going mad with excitement in the back of the car. They hadn't been on a call-out for a while, and had only been able to concentrate on training sessions, as Dave Riley was the training officer for SARDA. But Loch, like most of the old-timers, knew the difference.

The rain had set in steadily now, and Dave struggled into wet weather gear and attached Loch's special bell collar, which he used in preference to a jacket and coolight. Then he left the car parked at the bottom of the track and set off towards the base of the fell. Loch bounced away ahead of him, eager to begin, her collar jingling loudly. It was surprising how far away it could be heard: Dave could pick up her whereabouts up to a quarter of a mile away, even in bad weather.

The rain slanted down in the torchlight, turning the track into a sea of mud. There was no snow here, but as he turned off the track and splashed through the soaking bracken, he could see ahead the traces of snow at the edge of the crag. It would be warm work, climbing in this, especially in waterproofs. But at least there was a steady breeze blowing across the fellside, and Loch had already begun to quarter the thick cover at the fell bottom edge. She was an independent little dog, often ranging a long distance away, thinking for herself. It made her a valuable asset in poor visibility, when you were so much at the mercy of your dog. And nothing bothered her, neither rain nor high wind nor snow; she would still streak joyfully up the fellside with that fast, flowing movement of hers which made it all look so effortless.

*   *   *

Albert Bowness had been snoozing in front of the television all evening, the fire lit and the curtains drawn against the inhospitable night. It was getting late when he woke with a start and realised the time. He had to be up at six to take a lorry to the Midlands and there was the dog to take out. His wife was away at her sister's for a few days and it was surprising how things had got behind. And there seemed to be a week's washing-up to do before she got back.

He peered out of the window, suddenly aware that there seemed to be an awful lot of traffic on the road, headlights momentarily lighting up the curtains. There must be a 'do' on at the village hall tonight. He hoped they wouldn't finish too late, he had his sleep to think of.

He opened the front door. Rain slanted down into the light. He'd left the washing out. Why was everything so difficult? The dog was sitting at his feet, looking expectant. Blasted creature. Surely it didn't want a walk in this? The dog whined softly, his body shivering with excited antici-pation. He gave in and went to fetch the lead.

Curiosity led him along the narrow lane away from the village towards the village hall, where there certainly seemed to be a lot of activity. It was only a few yards round the bend, and if he walked back down the footpath he might be in time for last orders at the Dog and Pheasant (where the opening hours were very flexible) before they closed. Even from a few hundred yards he could see a blue flashing light. Hooligans, some of those disco people, chucking beer cans into his garden and singing in the small hours of the morning. Someone had probably had to call the police to eject them from the hall. About time too! He hoped it would teach them a lesson.

The whole car park was lit up, shadows going backwards and forwards. He stood on the grass verge, suddenly realising, as a car swept past, that he was standing beside Bill Wrightson from next but two. They nodded to each other, both bundled up to the eyeballs in mackintosh, scarf and cap.

'What's going on, then?' Albert shouted loudly. Bill was rather deaf at the best of times.

'Not often we see tha walking the dog!' Bill shouted back. 'The missus must be away on her holidays!'

Albert ignored the dig.

'What's going on, then? What are the police doin' here?'

'Seems that chap int village who does building fer council—tha knaws the fella. His grandfather did oop Hall fer owd Major Simpkin, him who was lost in the war . . . Well, he's lost oop on fell somewhere. Been there since yesterday back end, so I heard.'

'David Braithwaite, tha means?'

Bill Wrightson nodded lugubriously.

'Ay, that's the fella. Poor lad. Happen he ran away from that sharp-tongued mother-in-law of his.'

Albert was shocked.

'Nay, he's a nice lad, he is. How did he coom ter get hissel lost?'

'It's nay good asking me fer details,' Bill said gloomily. 'They nivver tell me owt round here. Think I'm simple. I'm jest off ter the pub fer a crack and ter see if anyone knaws owt. But they're that close round here, ah doot it!'

The two old men left the car park and made their way across the road to the footpath in search of gossip at the pub. After all, the landlord was in the team, and even if he wasn't there to pump for information, his wife might know something, and certainly Fred Brownrigg would be well informed from his place by the fire. It was not for nothing he was known as the village oracle.

*   *   *

Above them in the darkness, the long, patient search went on. Hour after hour of plodding upwards in the rain and slush, impeded by wet waterproofs, with rain running down the faces of the handlers, and the dogs drenched dark with water, the coats of the collies flattened by the downpour. It had been a long night for everyone, and there might be a long way to go. They were all hoping the rain would ease up, but if anything it grew heavier. The paths became miniature becks, hazardous to walk. What snow remained in the corries was only half solid, and higher up on the tops a couple of small avalanches had sprayed and tumbled down the steep slopes into the valley. Dave Brown, who had observed them from the valley side, resolved to take even greater care.

Down at HQ the team, in their own way, had been just as uncomfortable. Deprived of action, but nevertheless required to be on standby, many of them were trying to get a small amount of sleep either cramped up in cars and Land-Rovers or with sleeping bags and crash mats on the floor of the hall. Every few minutes a team member would come in or out of the door to report on a relay message, or reinforcements would arrive. The door, despite efforts to stop it slamming, would regularly reverberate with a sickening crash. You came to wait for it in the end, and while you might sleep through the voices and the sounds of the WRVS in the kitchen and a thousand other small distractions, there was no way you could sleep through the mind-bending explosion of the door meeting the frame at high speed. What was almost worse was the way everyone said 'Sorry' sheepishly, as the reverberations faded away, feeling as they must have done the waves of hatred coming at them from the groaning, cursing bundles in the corner of the hall. It was little things like that which drove you up the wall in the end.

At last some bright spark propped open the offending door, whereupon a draught of rain-laden Cumbrian air, liberally mixed with diesel fumes from the Land-Rover engines being run for warmth, made the floor even colder. But at least then you weren't being gassed to death by the heater. Look on the bright side . . . Mind you, if the door didn't get you, then there was always the phantom flusher which, just as sleep once more seemed within reach, would send the roaring sound of nineteen-thirties plumbing down the dank corridor from the Gents . . . after a while you could understand why MRTs are famed for their sense of humour. You wouldn't stay sane for long without it.

Along the valley floor most of the houses were now in darkness. All except one, where Ann Braithwaite sat out her lonely vigil. Spurning the offers from neighbours to sit with her, she made her pots of tea and waited by the phone, hoping against hope. Most other villagers, even those nearby, had no idea that a major search was going on on their doorstep.

*　　　*　　　*

The night wore on. The searchers were weary now, praying for the dawn. They were all, on their separate routes, approaching the great overhanging crag of Devil's Beak which, one way or another, must be negotiated before they could clear the paths to the summit. It had been decided that they would rendezvous on the plateau below Devil's Beak where the paths converged, and work out a plan of action.

Sam was very tired and getting bored, with hours of searching in the rain. Dawn was not far behind as they approached the Beak when, as so often happens in the fells, the weather suddenly changed. The last of the wet was whisked away as though by some efficient scene changer and it was replaced by clear skies with stars shining over the crag. There was still a bit of a moon, and a light, cold wind. John was aware that despite the waterproofs he was damp and chilled, the thin wind finding vulnerable spots where somehow the rain had got through. There might even be a frost before dawn, which would make the paths doubly lethal. You could rarely win with the weather, but in the meantime he was glad of the change and the improved visibility.

They stopped for a few moments in the shelter of rocks to drink and eat—John to gulp down still hot coffee and some chocolate which he shared with Sam, and Sam bounding off to drink from the stream.

He pressed the button on his radio.

'Dog Dominic from Dog John. Are you receiving me? Over.'

There was a crackle of static before Dom came back. The radios were unreliable at the best of times. They arranged to meet farther up, close to Monk's Ghyll where there was a waterfall coming straight down the crag.

John suddenly realised he could see, far below him, the lighted square which was the village hall car park, his area having worked back to the eastern side of the fell. Even though there were few car lights still on, and the hall lights had been dimmed, the visibility was now so good that he had no trouble looking straight down the valley and picking out HQ. He could even catch a glimpse of a distant lake glittering in the last of the moon. It was a beautiful night, but John suddenly felt the isolation of being a long way away from the centre of it all. He switched on his radio again. If he was in line of sight he would be able to report directly back to Control. Despite the two relays which Howard had set up, Dominic and John had been out of radio contact with Control for the duration of the search. It was time to report in.

'Wharbeck Control from Dog John. Are you receiving me? Over.'

'Dog John from Wharbeck Control. Receiving you strength five. Are you OK? Over.'

He was just about to make a routine report of his position when Sam came bounding back at him, jaws chomping excitedly.

'Wharbeck Control from Dog John. Hang on a minute. I seem to have a definite indication from Sam. Stand by. I'll follow it up.'

Sam was jumping up at him, mad with excitement. It had been a long night . . .

'Show me, Sam. Show me!'

Sam wheeled away off the path and scampered up the fell. John kept him in sight with the torch.

'Show me, Sam. Good dog. Show me!'

'Wharbeck Control from Dog John. We do seem to have definite indication . . . I repeat, stand by . . .'

He turned to face the valley for a moment and witnessed the dramatic effect of his words. Lights sprang into the dark and the beam of a powerful searchlight was switched on in the car park. The team would be awake now in readiness . . .

He turned and raced on upwards. Sam was standing on a flat-topped rock, barking fit to bust.

'Show me, Sam. Show me!'

Gasping for breath with the run up the fell, he scrambled over the rock. There was a stream and a shallow depression in the ground. The stench hit him. He shone his torch. It was a huge bloated shape. A dead sheep.

'Sam! How could you!'

He pressed the radio button.

'Wharbeck Control from Dog John. Many apologies. False alarm. Sorry to disrupt your beauty sleep . . .'

He would have to face the stick when he got back down . . .

'Sam! I know you were bored, but don't you EVER do that to me again. We'll be hung, drawn and quartered when we get back . . .'

Sam, his eyes showing red in the torchlight, didn't need a second telling. It had been a long, long night and he had been fed up and he wanted a game, but he knew he had blotted his copybook. He would never do it again. Promise. He came tentatively up to John and charged at his leg with his nose, his way of saying sorry.

'I know, old boy. You've worked hard. You need a break. We'll bivvy down for a while once we meet up with the others and we can both get some kip . . . just a bit longer. Away, Sam away. Good dog!'

Sam, hearing the change in his master's voice, galloped gaily up the fell again, eager to make up for his mis-demeanour, quartering the ground with new-found energy. But for the telling off, it had almost been worth it after all . . . !

It was a weary bunch of handlers who met at last, just as dawn was breaking, high up under Devil's Beak. The wind had died away completely but it was bitterly cold. There was a brief conference while they rested and had some food. There were more than enough of them to quarter the crag and the summit plateau and one of them would have to go down to speak for the Search Dogs at the Panel meeting. It was John's job as the SARDA representative to do so, so he was sent off down the hill with Sam, to face the long trek down the path.

He said goodbye to the others, having faced some chaff about Sam's false indication, and they made their dispirited way down the path. The others began the climb up the track which led to the ridge. They were all tired and cold.

Sam and John trudged down the hill. It had been a bad night and Sam was still in disgrace, and he knew it. He wanted to make up for his bad behaviour. John was sending him away in a half-hearted fashion. These were paths they had covered before. They were almost halfway down when the helicopter clattered along the valley floor, its powerful headlights cutting into the darkness. They stopped to watch it. Sam leaned his head against his master's knee. Both of them were miserable and cold.

The Panel meeting would begin as soon as the helicopter had landed. There would be an in-depth discussion about what to do next. The Search Dogs had covered almost the whole fellside, and found nothing. Now there was only the summit to search. If David Braithwaite wasn't there, a full line search would bring in Wharbeck team and probably other teams in the area for a massive, intensive search of the woodland areas.

A streak of red dawn came creeping frostily over the line of crags. If anything it grew colder. The fells seemed to stir into life. There were bird calls and soft movements in the bracken. Sam, who had been quartering the side of the fell, suddenly stood four-square, his ears pricked. The wind had died completely. They had strayed a little out of their own area, into a wedge of fell which was in between each of the assigned 'patches'. Then, without warning, Sam took off. John didn't take too much notice, but just went on trudging downwards. Sam was probably bored again, and there were rabbits in the bracken. He looked at his watch. If the helicopter had arrived, the Panel meeting would have begun, and they were still only halfway down. He pressed the button on his radio.

'Wharbeck Control from Dog John . . .'

Sam was up to him, barking madly, his jaws smacking together.

'Whoof! Whoof!'

Where had he been?

'Dog John from Wharbeck Control . . . receiving you . . .'

'. . . I was going to say, I'm on my way down, but I'll be late . . .'

'Whoof!' Sam was barking at him urgently . . .

'But just hang on . . .'

When things got exciting, one didn't always stick to the rules . . .

Search Dog Sam with
Brown at an
dale Search and
exercise.
Angela Locke

hil Haigh with Tosh
tired Search Dog
e.
Angela Locke

n 'Kipp' Brown,
Rossco
urtesy David Brown

25 Penny Melville (l
and Carol McNeill, w
their dogs Ben and K
Photo courtesy of PAL

26 Neil Powell of SA
Ireland, with Pepper, i
Newlands Valley. Un
the English SARDA
with their scarlet coa
the Irish dogs wear c
of emerald green.
Photo Angela Locke

A Penrith team
cise in Cawdale. One
alty' is found by a
with a broken leg . . .
Angela Locke

. . .and is bound tightly
stretcher before being
ed to safety.
Angela Locke

29 The other has **[had a]** heart attack and is g[iven] mouth-to-mouth resuscitation by Lar[ry] Meikle, after being wrapped warmly in a[plastic] sack.
Photo Angela Locke

30 The team ambu[lance] wait for the 'casualt[y] to be brought in.
Photo Angela Locke

'Not again, Sam! I couldn't stand it. You're not playing games again!'

'Whoof! Whoof! Come and see for yourself. Have I ever let you down? Well, not often . . .'

'OK, Sam. Show me. Show me.'

There was no wind. Sam was barking at a rockface. There was nothing there.

'I will NEVER . . . live this down!'

'Whoof! Whoof!'

'A bloody rabbit. It must be a bloody rabbit. We'll be finished now . . .'

'Dog John from Wharbeck Control . . . what's happening up there, John? You broke off in the middle of your transmission . . .

'. . . Just another false alarm . . .'

Rockface. Almost dark still, though the dawn light was on the high fell. Shine the torch. A small opening at the base of the rock. No wind. Sam couldn't have scented anything . . .

'Whoof!'

'OK I'll believe you, Sam. You just better . . .'

Paws up. GET ON WITH IT!!!!!

Squ.e.e.eze inside. A cave. He remembered suddenly, without looking at the map. There WAS a cave. Friar's Cave, Hermit's Cave . . . ? Something. Dark. Dark. Sam barking outside. No air. Panic. Dark. Where's the torch? Nothing here. It goes back. Sam doesn't know how to get in, just his nose.

A body was huddled at the very farthest corner of the cave, where it overhung the floor. Very still, half covered by a sports jacket. Was it alive? A good place to be, to survive, there might be a chance. John felt for a pulse. The eyes opened suddenly, pupils dilating in the torchlight. Clammy, cold skin on the wrist. Very sleepy. Bivvy sack out, empty out the rucksack. Spare sweaters, everything. Get Sam in here, put him in the bivvy sack. No injuries. Sam, it's all right. Just get in here, you daft old fool. Well done! Well done.

Squeeze out of the cave. How did he get in? He's a big bloke. It will have saved his life. Can't use the radio in there.

'Wharbeck Control from Dog John. Casualty located. Still alive. No injuries, conscious but suffering from hypothermia. Request team help immediately for medical aid and helicopter on standby . . .'

It was a dark, airless place but it was warmer than outside. Sam was put into the bivvy sack. A dog's body temperature is high enough to give heat gently . . . no hot water bottles, nothing too quick, for then the blood would rush to the extremities and the casualty could have a heart attack . . . But a dog, a bit smelly admittedly, old Sam, soft, quiet with his paws, not the first time he's been in a bivvy sack . . . knowing his job . . .

David Braithwaite had been clever enough. Wharbeck team, weary after their long night of waiting, were given new impetus. The crash party was up the fell in twenty minutes, administering the Reviva (the hot air machine for use with hypothermia) though one six-foot-six rugby-playing giant in the team couldn't get into the cave. But the hot air machine and Sam and simple comfort and a hot drink began to pull David Braithwaite back from that dangerous downhill slide towards sleep, from which there was usually no awakening.

It was a hard job getting him out of the cave, still only semi-conscious. There was no other entrance, and to this day, going back, David can't figure out how he found it the first time.

The helicopter thundered up the fell in the grey light, having landed and taken off again from the village hall field.

Two houses away, round the bend, Albert Bowness heard it in his sleep. The pub had been closed when the old boys had got there. He had never found out any more about what was going on. Meantime, he was tired out with all the chores. He spluttered and turned over and went back to his dream. Bill Wrightson snored away in the next house, oblivious. Only Fred Brownrigg, out to milk his two cows, looked up in surprise at the noise and watched the helicopter claw its way up the valley side . . .

It was full daylight now. The team had found a flat area of rock near the cave and manhandled the stretcher down. The helicopter hovered overhead, and then fell away as the winchman secured the casualty. David would be medivac-ed* to Carlisle for a couple of days' observation. The team watched as the stretcher swung up above them. There would be no lift down the fell today, they would have to walk. John was immeasurably weary, although Sam, convinced now that all was well and that he had redeemed himself, was racing about challenging Boris and any other dogs unwise enough to come near him.

Dogs and handlers and team members made their way down the tracks, hoping for hot soup and sandwiches and bed, at last.

By the time Mrs Gasgarth came out from the back to open up the village stores, and Terry Brass's Land-Rover came down the lane with the hay for the sheep, there was very little left to see . . . only a WRVS van being packed, and a team Land-Rover late away still being loaded. And by the time most folk were rousing themselves after a Sunday morning lie-in, to get down to the shop before it closed for lunch and they missed the papers, there was nothing at all to show for the night's activity . . . except a depression in the grass where the helicopter had landed and waited for its summons up the fell, an aroma of tomato soup and baked beans in the village hall, and a Kendal mint cake wrapper which a less than perfect citizen had lost from his rucksack in the dark, blowing across the grass . . .

Ann Braithwaite waited by her husband's bedside for him to wake up. She wanted to tell him something important . . . she didn't quite know yet how she was going to put it into words . . . but when he woke up, the words would come . . .

*Medical evacuation—in this case by helicopter.

7

INTERNATIONAL CALL-OUT

At twelve noon on 10th October 1986, the small, impoverished country of El Salvador in Central America was shaken to its very roots by great convulsions of the earth's crust. An earthquake had occurred which measured 5.4 on the Richter scale. Night after night, the television pictures showed the homeless wandering the streets of San Salvador, gathered in anxious groups around the rescue workers, hoping against hope that a mother, a father, a child, might still be living in the ruins.

The cameras scanned across the destruction: the toppled skyscrapers lurching over the narrow streets; the ruptured sewer pipes spreading their own insidious death from disease; the shanty buildings now no more than heaps of matchwood, a blanket stretched across the roof often the only shelter. We felt that same sense of impotence which the television coverage of such global tragedies produces for most of us. It was so far away, and what could we do? Only give a donation, and perhaps pray for the victims. What else was there . . . ?

*   *   *

Early autumn in Cumbria. Beautiful days of shimmering colour over the lakes, intensely blue skies, a blaze of early morning dew on the grass. A hard place to leave at any time. But in autumn, on mornings like these, hardest of all.

It was Saturday morning. Tina had taken the girls to a

dancing class in a village hall some distance away. Sam, drowsing in the sheltered sun, slept all tangled up with Tyan, among the pots of geraniums in the courtyard. He had managed to cut his paw badly only a few days before, and John was giving him a rest.

The phone rang as it was to ring that morning in a number of Saturday morning households, signalling pandemonium . . .

'John! It's a SARDA call-out . . .'

'OK. Where? I've got the map here . . .'

'San Salvador!'

'Very funny.'

'No, I'm serious. There's been a request from the International Rescue Corps. They're sending out a team of relief workers and they want a number of Search Dogs to go out with them. Two, we think. We're waiting for clarification on that. Flying out at nine o' clock tomorrow morning . . . but a decision by lunchtime today.'

'What? They can't possibly expect . . .'

'That's the message . . .'

'OK. I'll see what I can organise. I'll get back to you.'

John put the phone down slowly, his mind already racing ahead, trying to think out the practical problems . . . where was his passport? Was it even up to date? It was years since they had been abroad. And what about quarantine regulations? They would have to be waived before he could agree to go . . .

It was a big commitment. He had been sure instantly that he wanted to go. He too had been moved by the pictures on the news. To actually be able to do something. But the practical problems . . . with a family, with his job . . . How long would they be away? . . . To leave so soon . . . !

He must contact Tina. This would have to be a mutual decision. It was a lot to ask of her, too. But there was no phone in the village hall. And where in heaven's name was his passport? He spent a frustrating ten minutes looking for it. Tina would be away for hours, and what had they said? A decision by lunchtime. He had to give it his best effort, whatever happened . . .

*   *   *

Sergeant David Riley had been drafted in with other police from across Cumbria for duties at the Carlisle Football ground at Warwick Road. He was standing at the turnstiles, keeping an eye on the crowd as they filtered through. Suddenly he was jolted out of his thoughts by an urgent request on his pocket radio to contact Police HQ . . . He made his way to a telephone.

'Do you know how many policemen are likely to be involved in this San Salvador thing?'

Dave was mystified.

'There's been a request from International Rescue for SARDA dogs to help out in San Salvador . . . PC Shorrock from Patterdale has already volunteered . . . how many other SARDA members are likely to want to go . . . ?'

As soon as he could, Dave Riley rang Dave Brown, the SARDA secretary. Eighteen had volunteered so far, including John Brown. He added his name to the list. SARDA were still waiting for a decision from the Ministry of Agriculture about waiving quarantine on return to this country . . . they would just have to wait and see.

*   *   *

Tina had eventually been contacted through the good offices of the policeman's wife in the village, who had gone up to the hall to give Tina a message from John. Tina had come home at top speed, found the passport (out of date), but together they had decided that John must go if he were called. The only worry, which had begun to prey on John's mind, was Sam's cut paw. Would it be fair to take a dog halfway across the world to work in such gruelling conditions when he was even slightly under par?

*   *   *

By 6 p.m. the whole thing had begun to look like a game of Chinese Whispers. The message came through that no dogs were required after all from SARDA England. Two dogs from SARDA Wales, who had been contacted initially, were now in London awaiting a final decision on quarantine. As only two dogs would be needed, for everyone else the matter was closed.

John, still dazed by the whirlwind effort to get prepared in case of a call, was disappointed but also slightly relieved. That cut paw of Sam's had begun to loom large in his thinking with every hour that passed. And if there had been no waiving of quarantine, could any of them face the expense and the separation of six months in kennels when the dogs returned?

But David Riley, as SARDA Training Officer, was still in the front line . . .

It had been another of Sheila's splendid meals. He was feeling replete, relaxed, just in the mood to fall asleep in front of the television. It was often at this dangerous time that the phone would ring and it would be a call-out, somewhere inaccessible and nasty, just as it had started to rain. But the phone call which came at 9 p.m. was destined to call him much further away, and to a much hotter climate, where even the rain was lukewarm . . .

'Sheila! Quick, where's the atlas? You know—the one the lads used to use at school. I've got to know where San Salvador is . . . I've got to leave tonight!' MRT wives are known for their unflappability, policemen's wives equally so. But even so it took Sheila Riley a few minutes to absorb the idea fully.

'You'll need kit,' she said firmly, ticking things off on her fingers. 'I suppose it's rather hot there! But you haven't got anything like tropical gear. Just your old shorts from years back, and that tracksuit. You'll have to take that.'

'And dog food,' Dave interrupted. 'But just give me a

hand to find the place. I've got to know where I'm going! Jonesy wants me to ring him back. I don't know how I'm going to do it, but somehow I've got to get permission for two weeks' leave from work, sort my kit out, find out where and when the IRC wants us to meet . . .'

'So Dave Jones is going too, is he? What about the others?'

'They had to drop out because of quarantine regulations. The government won't lift them. Can't say I blame them. After all, it'll be pretty mucky over there . . .'

Somehow, miraculously, by 9.35 p.m. they had got it together. The Police Authority had given permission for leave to go to El Salvador, and the IRC had requested their presence by 9 a.m. the following morning at Marlow in Buckinghamshire! He was able to phone Dave Jones, at that time the secretary of SARDA Wales, and arrange to meet him on the M6 and to drive all night down to Marlow. There was no time for second thoughts, just a few moments to pack and make final arrangements. As Sheila had suggested, light tropical gear was in rather short supply in the Riley household, and Dave had also only managed to rustle up one tin of dog food and a packet of dog biscuits. After all, it was late and the shops were shut. He didn't think the shopkeepers would be too sympathetic to being knocked up and asked for emergency supplies for El Salvador! He had very little money on him and had grabbed his credit card as an afterthought, not sure whether it would even be of any use. As it turned out it proved invaluable.

Jonesy had told him over the phone that they were to be billeted in a good-class hotel away from the earthquake area, so the only necessary equipment would be the aforementioned light tropical gear and a decent pair of trousers (Why? he wondered. Would they be expected to join the social circuit?) as well as dog food for a fortnight. He had at least managed to produce a suitable pair of trousers. For the rest he would have to rely on his own skills, most important of all his dog, and a certain amount of improvisation.

The two Davids reached Marlow at 8 a.m. the following morning. Eventually, after making enquiries at an early morning newsagent, they found the headquarters of the International Rescue Corps—a semi-detached house in a quiet residential suburb.

Dave Jones went off to make contact, leaving Dave Riley to mind the vehicle. He came back looked rather worried.

'I don't know how to break this to you, David. This is serious. The IRC just gave me a roasting. Asked me whether we had our sleeping bags, cooking equipment, water bottles, eating utensils and all other necessities for living rough. I had to tell him we were a bit short in that quarter and he got rather excited . . . I couldn't bring myself to say that we had been expecting to be put up in a "good-class hotel". Perhaps after all that was a trifle optimistic!'

Dave Jones had managed to scrounge a couple of pairs of overalls and two sleeping bags, but for the rest they were on their own.

'Oh, and by the way,' he continued, 'We can only take one piece of luggage.'

Any unsuspecting early morning jogger pacing the suburban roads of Marlow that morning might have been a trifle startled by the sight of two men (watched by two puzzled collies) dressing and undressing down to their underpants, trying on various combinations of sports trousers, tracksuits, shorts and shirts, in order to decide what might possibly be stuffed into a single bag. What, after all, would be the right gear for two weeks as part of a rescue team in an earthquake zone? Neither of them could do more than hazard a guess, and hope for the best. Dave Riley was convinced that at any moment the police would turn up, having received a complaint from the local residents, with all the embarrassment that might involve!

It was a frustrating and somewhat farcical beginning. Things could only get better, and in fact, much to the two dog handlers' relief, the IRC proved to be a very efficient organisation, well experienced in disaster response, with experience in both the Colombian and Mexican earthquakes; a registered charity whose brief was to send a team with the minimum delay anywhere in the world at a few hours' notice, where skilled help might be required.

At Heathrow the fourteen-man team was met by a bevy of photographers and journalists. British Airways had agreed to pay the cost of travel, which was considerable, and already public interest had been aroused. The Search Dogs were the subject of particular attention. It was the first time many people had heard the term 'search dog', and had begun to appreciate the work of SARDA's usually unsung heroes.

In the meantime, the worrying business of finding the correct crates for two such special animals and preparing them for the long haul over the Atlantic kept the two handlers busy. By midday all was prepared. The team were given VIP treatment at every stage, and the two Davids were amazed at the number of procedures and regulations which the IRC organisers had managed to sweep away within a few hours of the earthquake. The trip could never have taken place without such a phenomenal back-up.

'This will be the longest call-out you've ever been on, Riley boy!'

David Jones closed his eyes and stretched out on the seat of the jumbo jet bound for Miami. Dave Riley grinned. It was hard to get used to. A little over twelve hours ago he had been sitting down to dinner at home, still largely unaware of the hurricane which was heading his way. They were both exhausted after the events of the last twelve hours, but it was hard to relax and sleep. They were keyed up now with anticipation, and at least they were on their way! He couldn't wait to get there and begin.

The IRC, with enormous efficiency, had taken care of everything, firstly on the 'hop' to Miami, and then the next leg with Challenge Airways out to San Salvador. It meant the team could be fit and ready when they finally arrived, without worrying about all the details of travelling halfway round the world.

There was a few hours' stop-over in Miami, and Dave Riley and Dave Jones were able to unload the dogs and give them a good walk. It was a great relief to see that the animals seemed quite unperturbed by the experience so far; even the noise and bustle of an international airport didn't seem to upset them at all.

And when they finally arrived at their destination, jet-lagged and somewhat bemused, at 2.20 a.m., the dogs greeted them exuberantly. It was a great adventure, after all! Once all the formalities had been gone through Loch settled happily at her master's feet for the truck ride into the city. But it was already boiling hot, and Dave Riley couldn't help wondering how the dogs would fare when the sun came up and it became even hotter. Would they be able to operate in tropical heat, and how would they cope after the disorientating effects of the long journey through several time zones?

The first sight of El Salvador in the early light was far from reassuring. Army personnel were wandering about everywhere carrying loaded rifles. There was an atmos-phere of tension. (They were soon to learn that the political situation was dangerously unstable. Many of the El Salvadorian people were in revolt against the military government.) Everywhere, too, there were signs of earth-quake damage, although the epicentre was some miles away. Great cracks had opened up in the road surfaces and many roads were blocked because of landslides.

But it was still beautiful countryside, green after the rainy season. San Salvador, the capital, was 2,200 feet above sea level. It was even now a gracious city of flowers and trees. Despite the devastation they were to find at its centre, the traffic was flowing after a fashion, and people were carrying on their everyday lives in the shanty towns which bordered the highways.

Dawn was breaking as they arrived at the luxurious Sheraton Hotel, which was overlooked by a volcano. It seemed that the original briefing had been partly right! The hotel was surrounded by exotic coconut palms; brightly-coloured birds flew about in the trees. No wonder this country had been for so long the playground of rich America. The tranquil swimming pool and the thatched drinks bar gave a final touch of unreality, after the drive through the earthquake devastation . . .

All about the grounds people were sleeping on sun beds and mattresses. At first the two handlers assumed the heat was driving them to spend the nights outside, but very quickly they found that daily tremors were shaking the hotel, and most people were afraid to sleep indoors.

In the circumstances, their temporary camp in the basement of the hotel seemed rather risky, and in fact by the Wednesday the whole hotel was declared structurally unsafe and they were forced to move camp to the swimming pool chalets, which were rather cramped and leaked when it rained, but beat camping outdoors by a long chalk!

The crates in which the dogs had flown halfway round the world were set up as kennels. The two Border Collies had already become a centre of attention from the world's press, and photographers were to pursue them wherever they went. But the dogs remained for the most part unflappable, even during the worst of the days which were to come.

That first morning, after briefing, the team set out for the city centre. It soon became obvious that San Salvador was a very dangerous place to be, and not only because of the constant earthquake tremors, the risk of another major 'quake', the threat of collapsing buildings, the possibility of disease and the like. Political tension was everywhere, and as so many separate countries had sent teams out to the disaster area, there was at times a lack of overall co-ordination which was positively life-threatening. At one point they found themselves working on one side of a building, crawling through the layers to look for anyone who might be trapped but still alive, when they became aware that a team from another country had started working with a bulldozer on the other side, at a moment when the slightest vibration was threatening to bring down the whole house of cards on the struggling rescuers.

The dogs had been trained to locate people on the airborne scent from the body. The two handlers had no idea how Meg and Loch would react in such different circumstances, where there were so many human scents around, so much noise and dust, and very little wind—only the odd draught filtering through the broken buildings. Both men were apprehensive.

On that first morning Dave Riley joined forces with another team member. The building to which they had been assigned had collapsed in a wedge shape, the first floor having dropped to ground level at one end. It was obvious from the smell that at that point a dead body was trapped under the huge weight of the superstructure. But there might be others alive on the far side of the building, although a team of Swiss Search Dogs had already made an initial foray into the darkness.

They crawled inside. It was pitch black, the tilting floor a swathe of broken glass. Even orientation was difficult. Perspectives, in this sickening, lurching world, had been twisted out of all recognition. Loch, moving quietly, was ahead of him.

Together they crawled inch by inch into the heart of the building, to where once there had been a men's outfitting shop. Was it possible that anyone could still be alive in this devastation?

Suddenly, out of the murk, they were faced with a horrifying sight a few inches from their faces. Strangely, Loch had not reacted, but there, directly in front of them was a collection of arms and legs strewn about with seemingly reckless abandon. Dave shone the torch round, and as realisation dawned on them the tension was broken for a few moments. What they had unwittingly chanced upon were the remains of the display dummies from the tailor's shop!

They had a similar fright a few moments later when, searching through the baker's shop in the same complex, they came across the contents of a smashed jar of jam spread across the sloping floor, gleaming crimson in the torchlight. There was a burst of relieved laughter. The same ability to find humour in the grimmest situations had seen Dave Riley through many a traumatic rescue in the past. It is always there, as part of the protective armour of all MRT members. It enables them to cope, when others might have gone under. Now it was especially valuable.

The search of the first building proved fruitless. They emerged blinking in the brilliant sunlight, weary and tense. Anxiously, Dave bent down to examine Loch's paws. All that broken glass! But miraculously, the dog's tough pads, built up over long hours of searching on scree slopes in the Lakes, and the granite faces of the crags, had stood her in good stead. She didn't have a single cut. And all the time they were in San Salvador, despite the hazardous job they were doing, both dogs somehow escaped being injured.

At the end of the day they climbed onto the truck for the rather unnerving journey back to the hotel. The hair-raising drives back and forth through the chaotic San Salvador traffic, weaving at high speed round the giant cracks and the piles of rubble in the road, seemed as dangerous as anything else they might encounter. The San Salvadorian drivers seemed to work on the principle of finding a gap in the traffic, putting their foot down, closing their eyes and hoping for the best!

Everywhere were the cheerful brown faces of the people, still able to laugh despite everything. It was good to feel that they were giving something back. The El Salvadorian people are of Spanish extraction, and speak Spanish. The poverty of most of the population, and the gap between the rich and poor, coupled with the uncertain political future, had made life difficult enough. Now the earthquake had shattered so many lives, and killed so many, leaving families bereft of support or homes to live in. The wonder was that they could smile at all. Everywhere there were the guns and the drab uniforms of the soldiers, contrasting strangely with the bright flowers which still bloomed lavishly in the gardens of ruined hotels and houses.

Dust, noise, palm trees, blue sky, political tensions; the smell of death everywhere. Dave Riley found himself longing sometimes for the quiet tranquillity of his own mountains, for the bracken changing to red-gold now in autumn; for the sharp frosts, the familiar shape of the Langdales rearing up over Elterwater; for the forest paths above Windermere. Nevertheless, they were doing a good job, and it was an exciting place to be. Above all, it was a challenge for the whole team.

The swimming pool was a boon. After another day crawling through dust and debris, surrounded by the stench of trapped bodies, to be able to come back, strip off and plunge into the pool was absolute bliss.

But as the days crawled by, the heat made searching more hazardous and unpleasant. They had been given a cholera jab on the Monday morning but the possibility of widespread disease across the city was becoming daily more likely. There were large numbers of bodies trapped in the ruined city, and as time passed, they made their presence felt. How could Loch and Meg possibly find a living human scent in the midst of everything? It was so very different from the clean, fresh, windswept air of the fells and mountains.

The dogs were astonishing. They seemed to adapt with hardly a problem. Somehow, it was as though they were still working their own 'patch'—the fells and the Yorkshire moors for Loch, the Snowdon range for Meg. In situations like these the years of training, and of thinking for themselves, showed up in the character and stamina of

SARDA dogs. And Loch, just over a year later, was to prove herself again as a 'survivor' in very different circumstances . . .

Meg and Loch were truly part of the IRC team, and a valuable addition to it, required to do some very difficult work. Not only did they have to get used to the 'scent' of a dead body and separate it out from that of a living one, they had also to work in conditions of great human tension and danger.

One of the hotels, the Gran, had been rocked by a tremor on the first afternoon, while three of the team members were carrying out a search in the basement. There could be no immediate escape, and the searchers had no alternative but to sit tight and wait for the building to 'settle'. It was a pale and subdued group who eventually emerged into daylight. They had had their first encounter with the very real risk of a fatal accident which they must live with every day.

Loch and Meg would be sent ahead of their handlers, crawling through narrow cracks in the dark, using their marvellous, 'scenting' abilities, with the handler squeezing in behind them, giving instructions. On one occasion Meg was held to David Jones' chest while he was lowered down a manhole, in order to gain access to the lower levels of a collapsed building. The two dogs were the only collies working in the disaster area. The Swiss, innovators in Search Dog techniques, used Alsatians, and the two British handlers were interested to see the Swiss abseiling across the broken buildings with their massive dogs draped over their shoulders. All the dogs were doing wonderful work, but the collie handlers were sometimes grateful for the smallness of their own dogs, which enabled them to squeeze through narrow entrances where other dogs might have had difficulty.

On the Tuesday morning, the whole team were transported to the main disaster area, the Ruben Dario building. This was a huge complex housing a cinema, shops, offices

38 Sam on the fells at
night. After a long search
in the cold and dark, an old
dog finds it easier to bivvy
down with his master for a
few hours, rather than
making the long trek back
down to Base.
Photo courtesy John Brown

39 Search Dog Sam – on
the call-out list until the
very end.
Photo courtesy John Brown

Chad, the boxer who
s found, after being lost
two weeks in a remote
t of the Cleveland
ors, by trainee collie
ch, with his little West
ghland companion.
to courtesy of owner

The author visiting
Incident HQ at
llingham Police Station,
ich became the Control
ntre for the search of
elder Forest after the
ckerbie disaster. Tail
tions of the Pan Am
eing 747 had fallen over
vide area of the forest.
to courtesy Brian Wright

34   Once in the helicopt
most dogs, like Sam, ar
content to settle down .
Photo Angela Locke

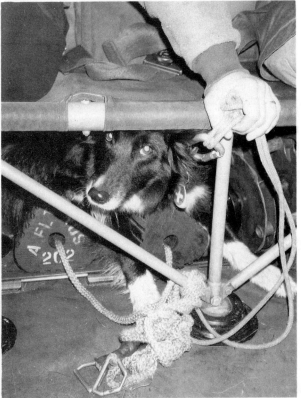

35   . . . but Alison Cola
collie Nell dives straigh
under the seat and rema
there for the duration c
the flight.
Photo Angela Locke

31 A helicopter familiar-
sation weekend hosted by
Cleveland Search and
Rescue Team. The dogs
are encouraged to walk all
round and into the
helicopter . . .
Photo Angela Locke

32 & 33 . . . before being
winched up into the
airborne aircraft, an
experience that Sam
endures unwillingly but
stoically.
Photos Angela Locke

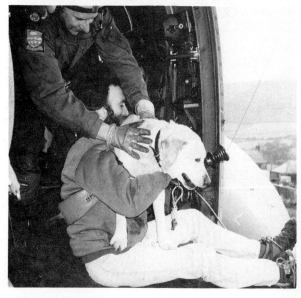

and a large dental practice. It was estimated that there could be between 300 and 400 people trapped inside. Tensions were mounting between the teams. The Swiss rescue workers had been working on the building since Day One. There had been a terrible fire which had raged for three days after the earthquake, making the work even more dangerous and difficult.

Now teams from six more countries were directed to work on the complex and the Americans were put in overall charge by the rescue co-ordination centre. A dispute broke out over this and most of the day was wasted while attempts were made to resolve the situation. The team waited in the tropical heat, fuming at the delay. Every once in a while a crowd would gather, to be driven back with the San Salvadorian method of crowd control observed before by Dave Riley—a rope end swept into the densest part of the groups to keep them back. It wasn't until the evening that the dogs and men were put to work, elsewhere in the city. Everyone was fed up and frustrated.

But the next day brought a real sense of achievement. Faint cries for help had been heard coming from the building they had searched on Monday. Electronic sounding equipment was brought in, and, incredibly, seemed to indicate that there might be someone still alive inside.

Loch was sent in and asked to 'find'; and much to everyone's amazement, she indicated several times at the place where the building had collapsed onto the pavement. It was known there was a dead body under the super-structure at this point, but her indications were quite clear, and eventually it was decided to remove a section of the concrete canopy. The Guatemalan Fire Brigade arrived and began working. Dave and Loch, their job done, were sent on with the rest of the team to another site on the far side of the city.

It wasn't until the afternoon that a message came over the CB radio. A man had been found alive, in a tiny space no more than two feet deep, at the point where Loch had indicated. A dead woman was beside him. He had probably survived by drinking the water from a fractured water pipe.

It was a source of quiet satisfaction to have found someone alive after so long, and to know the dog was still able to use her skills as effectively as she had so often done on her 'home' territory, despite all the stresses, the alien smells, the dust and the absence of a clean wind. But this was a team effort, and Dave and Loch were part of it. If there were credits they were for the work they had all put in, both nationally and internationally, in the effort to save lives.

It had been a good day, nonetheless, and the news that the government had given permission for the team to be fed from the restaurant at the hotel made everyday conditions much easier, and added to a great boosting of morale. Since their arrival the IRC had survived on issues of 24-hour ration packs from the Army. There weren't enough funds available to buy food.

Over the next two days, the team certainly needed any boosts they could find. The work became increasingly dispiriting. Later that evening the whole team were called back to the Ruben Dario building where the problems of who was to take charge had finally been resolved. Until the Thursday evening they worked in shifts, directed by the Americans, in temperatures well over 100°F. Many bodies wre found but only one was still alive, and he died before reaching hospital.

It was harrowing work, which was becoming more saddening with the passing of time. Only a miracle would have enabled anyone trapped in the ruins to survive after such a long time. Even worse was the task to which they were assigned on the Friday. The university campus had been extensively damaged in the earthquake, but no search had been carried out until that day. A local guide was of the opinion that this particular university was considered a 'nest of rebels' by the government and thus somewhat low on the list of priorities for help. Needless to say, no one was located alive.

The stresses and tensions of searching in such difficult conditions were beginning to tell. On one day of intense heat Loch turned her face to the wall and 'went on strike', and in a moment of totally uncharacteristic bad temper, bit David Jones on the hand.

It was becoming obvious to the whole team that any further work in San Salvador would only be of a demolition nature; there would be no more chance of finding anyone left alive. So on the Friday evening it was decided to return home. Attempts to find accurate casualty figures were frustrated on all sides. They were told that the most reliable source of information would be the British press reports!

On Saturday, 18th October, they flew home, enjoying the same VIP treatment they had experienced on the way out, including being entertained by the Miami Airport Fire Brigade for the day, *en route*. At 11 a.m. on the Monday they arrived back, battle-weary and somewhat dazed, to a bevy of reporters at Heathrow.

The dogs were to be taken off the plane by quarantine officials and taken into isolation immediately. There was no putting off the partings any longer. The moment both handlers had dreaded since the day they had volunteered to go out to El Salvador was now upon them. Loch and Meg, who had done so much for them, had been so brave, had performed so well, must now be parted from their handlers for six months. The rules were essential: El Salvador was rife with rabies, and either dog could be incubating it. But the parting would not be any easier for all that.

The two handlers were given wellington boots and overalls and made to walk through a disinfectant area before they were able to greet their dogs after the flight, and as quickly say goodbye to them for half a year. It didn't do to look at it like that. Dave Riley made a big fuss of Loch in her kennel, and then walked determinedly away. It would do no good for the dog to be upset more than necessary, but it was very hard.

Looking back later, Dave was just grateful that they were still so caught up in it all that he could see it as a part of the necessary routine of coming home. It was only later that the full sense of loss would hit them both.

The bill for quarantine, they discovered, would be £1,000 each. It was with considerable relief that the two handlers had learned that Pedigree Petfoods, makers of PAL, who had recently begun considerable sponsorship of SARDA England, would pay the bill for Loch. And Charlie Watts, drummer with The Rolling Stones, telephoned the next day and generously offered to pay the bill for Meg's stay in kennels. It was one less thing to worry about and they were very grateful.

The dogs had proved themselves over and over again as life-savers, whether quartering the ground in snow looking for lost walkers in snow and ice, or crawling through narrow tunnels in stifling heat searching for earthquake victims. But more than anything else, they were valued friends. The days ahead would be very long indeed until they could all be reunited again . . .

For Dave Riley the whole El Salvador experience is something he will never be able to forget. He found himself, for a long time after the traumatic events of that week, still unable to think about anything else. The scale of death, the extent of the tragedy, the intensity of that week-long period, was sometimes hard to come to terms with. While they were there, working until they were too tired to think, obeying team orders, doing their best, there was no time to reflect. They were on the spot and there was a job to be done. But coming home, the full implications of the earthquake hit him hard.

And for the six months that Loch was away, although Dave concentrated on bringing on another pup, everything seemed somewhat out of joint. Until he could take to the fells again with his beloved dog quartering the mountainside ahead of him, life would never quite be back to normal . . .

*   *   *

At a dinner on 24th January, 1988, held for the presentation of the PRO-Dog of the Year awards at the Grosvenor Rooms in North London, Loch was presented with the PRO-Dog Gold Medal Award for Life-Saving. The charity's citation read: 'For the saving of human life in the El Salvador earthquake disaster.'

At that same ceremony Meg was awarded the Gold Medal Award for Devotion to Duty. the citation read: 'For rescue work following the El Salvador earthquake disaster.' The charity stated:

> The Devotion to Duty and Life-Saving medals this year are unique in that they are awarded for exceptional deeds performed far from these shores and are intended to honour not only two brave British dogs but dog teams from many lands who do such valuable work in finding people buried alive in the aftermath of earthquakes.

On the evening that the awards were confirmed, Meg was out on an emergency call in the Welsh hills with her handler. She was by then a veteran of eleven years, and she would never be asked to go abroad again, but at the time of writing her working ability remains unimpaired.

As for Loch, two weeks and one day later, she was once again to become headline news . . .

8

'THE WORST WEATHER FOR TWENTY YEARS'

February 1988 . . . It had already been a bad week. When the snow comes to the North like that, perhaps only every four or five years, it can come with a vengeance. Three people had been blown off the tops in the Cheviots, and all across the North the MRT teams were swinging into action . . .

Langdale/Ambleside base, alongside the main road, was a hive of activity. There had already been a call-out late on Friday night, and on Saturday afternoon there was a second call-out to Tarn Crag, where a man from Ambleside had fallen 80 feet down a snow gully. It involved taking a Team Land-Rover and walking up from Dunmail Raise in ever-deepening snow. At one stage a Team Land-Rover had to be hauled out of the snow by a farmer with his tractor. Luckily the man was found where he was expected and the MRT carried him down by stretcher into Patterdale, a long stretcher-carry in worsening conditions.

On Sunday afternoon, a lone walker fought his way through deep snow to Troutbeck Park Farm, halfway up the Troutbeck valley, arriving exhausted and half-frozen. On his way down he had come across three men, too worn out to move any farther, huddled together under the lee of a stone wall. In the near-blizzard conditions they had become disorientated, and were waiting and hoping that the storm would ease. But it was getting worse by the hour. The walker had promised to try and get help and, himself in a bad way, had managed to make his way down to the farmhouse.

The farmer and his wife were well used to the valley being the scene of mountain rescue operations. It was a favourite spot for walkers, but could be lethal in bad winter conditions. Luckily the telephone was still working . . .

It was Dave Riley's weekend off duty—Friday to Monday. He had been looking forward to some peace. Perhaps he would get a chance to watch a film on TV, play with his little daughter, Charlotte, spend some time with the family. The night-and-day shift pattern of his work as a police sergeant in Kendal left little time for relaxation. But already it had been a hard couple of days. Perhaps Sunday, after all, would prove to be quiet. He decided to take Loch up into the fells in the morning, to catch up on some snow training. It was always important to keep the dog up to scratch, particularly in bad conditions. You never knew when you might need her to be stretched to the limit . . .

His wife Sheila was a wonderful cook. To come back from a morning in the snow to his house in Windermere and smell that mouth-watering Sunday lunch was a moment to savour . . . and to be able to relax in front of the television in a warm house, replete with good food. But it was tempting fate to count your blessings, to get too comfortable . . .

He was just slipping into a comfortable doze when the MRT pager which he carried on his belt went off with a shrill bleep, startling him out of his half-sleep. Loch, dozing in front of a warm fire, lifted her head, instantly alert. If the bleep went, it was an MRT rescue. They would be paging her master from the team base. A SARDA call-out would have involved a phone call, but Loch hoped she would still be taken along, just in case.

'Sheila, it's a team call-out! I'd better get a move on!'

But his wife, after twenty years as a Mountain Rescue wife, had her ears finely tuned for the bleeper. She was already halfway to the kitchen to make up a flask of hot Ribena.

'You can take a bit of this quiche,' she shouted back. 'And your socks are still drying on the radiator.'

He raced upstairs and started pulling out dry clothes from the cupboard. By the time he came down the stairs two at a time, Loch was waiting at the bottom, amber eyes fixed appealingly on her master, the long brush of her collie tail sweeping the carpet. There was no way she was going to be left behind.

Sheila was waiting with his flask and food. She had enough confidence in Dave not to worry too much. After all those years you would have ended up a nervous wreck if you did.

But as Dave opened the door and she saw the depth of snow on the front step and on the car bonnets in the road, and felt the icy draught of air which swept through the hallway, she had a twinge of apprehension. A lot of snow must have fallen since they sat down to lunch and now the wind was getting up again . . .

Dave stood in the doorway, fastening his coat.

'We had better get a move on,' he said. 'Whoever is out in this will be having a bad time of it.'

Charlotte came toddling up to give him a hug.

'Take care, Daddy. Take care!' she said firmly. They all laughed, and she planted a kiss on Loch's head before marching off again.

'Shut the door quickly. You'll lose all the heat.'

He was already halfway down the path. Sheila shouted goodbye and fought to shut the door in a sudden gust of snow-laden wind. Whoever was out on the hill, she felt very sorry for them.

Windermere, so crowded with visitors in the summer-time, was like a ghost town, the streets virgin white under the falling snow. Many roads were beginning to be cut off, and no one was going out unless they had urgent business. It was a struggle to get the five miles to Langdale/Ambleside base, although driving in bad conditions was second nature now. The snow flung itself against the side of the car in bursts of rage. The wind whipped the lakeside black and torn, sending spray up onto the road.

The red clock in the base had been stopped at 4.25 p.m., the call-out time. It was full dark by now. The base was crowded, the windows steaming up against the cold. A Land-Rover was being loaded in the forecourt, and Dave, after getting a briefing from the team leader, piled into the back with the others, Loch as usual almost on his lap. They would be glad of the winter tyres and the chains which kept a grip on the slippery surface as they swayed their way up the road towards the Troutbeck valley.

It had seemed bad down by the lakeside, but up in the fells it was much worse. A 'crash', or advance, party, made up of team members who lived near enough to the base to get away first, had already set off towards Threshwaite Cove, carrying emergency supplies. The rest of the team split into several parties, Dave with Loch and some team members taking one side of the valley and other team members going up the other side, in case the lost walkers had become separated. It was hard searching, the snow piled in deep drifts, sometimes over the path. Loch's lightness was a boon here. She could pick her way over the snow without being buried. Dave had put on her bell collar and it could be clearly heard, even above the howl of the wind.

At last, over the radio, the news came through that the party had been located, and all search parties made their way to the valley side where the three figures were lying in the snow. They were all in a fairly bad way, although not injured. The crash party had put an emergency bivvy over them and one of the team doctors was administering the Reviva, the hot air machine. They were all suffering from hypothermia. Hours of walking in severe conditions in a killer wind, combined with thick snow and the bitter cold, had sapped their vital energy and lowered their body temperature, taking a dangerous toll.

The crash team had noted that the worst affected casualty had been so confused by hypothermia that his wet weather gear was still in his rucksack. This was what happened: people became confused as the blood supply to the brain was affected, and would often not be able to take the actions of basic survival.

The conditions by now were approaching white-out. A helicopter would have been impossible, and as the warming effects of the Reviva and food and glucose began to be felt by the casualties, it was decided that once the three men had sufficiently recovered, they could safely be walked down to the farm.

It took hours, and it was well after midnight when the lights of the farm at last came into view. They were all exhausted and wet and cold. The farmer and his wife, Mr and Mrs Tyson, were waiting for them anxiously, and as the door was opened into the kitchen a delicious smell of baking stole out into the frozen night.

'You timed it well! It's baking day today—yesterday, I should say now! So I've put on a bit of a tea for you!'

It was traditional at Troutbeck Park Farm. No matter what the hour, when they came down off the hill chilled and tired and after hours of searching or stretcher-carrying, a wonderful spread would be waiting for them. Even the casualties revived when they saw the newly baked food laid out on the kitchen table. It was crammed end to end with scones and pies and pastries. Loch stationed herself under the tablecloth looking hopeful. They all realised suddenly how desperately hungry they were.

The operation had taken eight hours and had involved twenty-seven team members. It had been a success. The team doctor checked all the casualties again and pronounced them out of danger. They were free to tuck in!

It was the early hours and bitterly cold before Dave eventually tiptoed quietly up to bed, peeling off wet and snowy gear as he went. It had been an exhausting weekend so far. Would he now be able to catch up on that long-awaited sleep? It might be tempting fate again to hope so . . .

* * *

John Brown's team, too, had been involved in a dramatic rescue of their own that day . . .

Two pairs of walkers had set off separately, early on Sunday morning, in what had been good conditions, with a blue sky and very little wind. They were all well-equipped for winter walking, with ice axes and crampons, essential for any expedition into the fells in snow and ice. Close to the summit, without warning, both parties had encountered the sudden, terrifying onslaught of 50 to 60 mile an hour winds. Blizzard conditions had set in with unbelievable ferocity. It was an almost continuous white-out. Someone later described it as a 'concrete wall of snow' advancing across the slopes. Combined with the almost hurricane force wind and an extreme drop in temperature, these were killer conditions.

Both parties, separately, had decided to make the descent by the safest route, avoiding the exposed ridge, but as they felt their way through the impenetrable spindrift, both met with the same fate. Massive cornices had built up on the edges of the crags, often extending the path outwards by twenty or thirty feet of apparently solid snow—death traps in this visibility.

Both leaders in each two-man expedition had suddenly found the ground giving way from under them, and they were literally hurled into space, to fall many feet below onto a precipitous slope. To attempt to brake with their ice axes was futile, while their crampons only made things worse, catching in the snow and sending them head over heels against hidden rocks, at a terrifying speed . . . Their partners were left in the howling whiteness, shouting in vain, and with increasing hopelessness. Then they each set off by different routes to attempt to get help. But the chances seemed slim of even getting down off the mountain, let alone being in time.

*   *   *

John had been laid up all weekend with a bad back, an enduring memory of that terrible night a few years ago, when he had carried an injured Sam down the mountainside. He knew that out on the hill he would be more of a liability than an asset . . . all he could do was rest, and fume with frustration.

But by Sunday lunchtime it had become too much for him. He had just been ferrying Matthew to play with a friend, thinking about the team out on the hill, wondering how they were getting on with the snowcraft exercise they had planned. The weather was certainly getting worse. Intermittently, he managed to pick up the 'crack' over the radio, relayed back to Base. He heard the team leader order everyone off the hill. Then suddenly there was pandemonium. Messages were flying backwards and forwards . . . something about walkers being blown off the ridge, someone had fallen through a cornice . . . What on earth was going on?

He decided then and there that he had to go and give a hand. After all, he could still drive a Land-Rover, and it sounded as though the team were going to need all the help they could get . . .

*   *   *

It was a spectacular landscape. Cornices shelved out from the crag, defying the laws of gravity. The weather was unpredictable, but there were intervals of almost perfect blue sky and sunshine. Occasionally they paused in their work to enjoy the dramatic beauty of it all. The team had gained a lot that morning, about how to function in deep snow. It would be valuable experience when the real thing came along. Little did they realise how soon that would be.

Some of the team members were working along a footpath below the ridge. They had had lunch in a sheltered spot under the crag and now they were doing some snow training with one of the trainee search dogs.

Suddenly, without warning, the weather hit. It was a white-out with a blasting, gale force wind throwing up spindrift in their faces, so that they were temporarily blinded. In failing light, they began to prepare to evacuate the hill. The wind was strengthening to a point where in exposed places they had the greatest difficulty keeping their footing. Then, just as the team leader had called for all personnel to rendezvous at the base of the fell, a flying figure appeared in the mist, sliding and falling through the deep snow from above. He was shouting against the wind.

'Help! Help! My friend . . . he's fallen through a cornice. Please help. I think he's dead!'

They fought their way over to him. The wind was at screaming pitch by now; they had to make themselves understood by gesturing. As they climbed on up, a man came running towards them in the gloom. He was badly shocked and they had some trouble establishing his identity. Eventually they realised that this was the casualty whose friend had come running down to them to raise the alarm. He had indeed fallen through a cornice, and somehow survived almost unscathed. He had tried to dig himself a snow hole after he had fallen, but had rapidly realised that although he was suffering minor injuries, he would be better off trying to make his way down. His hands were badly cut, but otherwise, miraculously, he seemed almost unhurt.

A team member was detailed to escort him off the hill, where he could be given treatment for shock and have his hands dressed. Then over the radio came the message that a man had been blown off the ridge somewhere above them. The first of the uninjured ridge walkers had managed to get down from the mountain onto the road below and raise the alarm. All team members in the area were requested to help. Those remaining fought their way upwards, the snow shifting under them.

Then, almost, unbelievably, another message came through on the radio. A second person, they now heard, had been blown off the ridge, in an almost identical situation. His partner, too, had by now struggled to the local team base at Patterdale to raise the alarm. The cliché that all hell had broken loose seemed only too apt. Experienced walkers with all the right equipment were being caught by a deadly combination of cornice and freak wind and white-out conditions. The fellside at that moment was one of the most dangerous places in England, and woe betide any foolish mortal who dared to challenge the elements . . .

It was best not to dwell on the possibility of avalanches, which could be heard roaring down the far slope of the mountain. With the snow as unstable as it was, and the gale force wind which howled like a banshee through the huge cornices under the crag, anything might happen. The radio was crackling into life continuously with emergency messages.

The first seriously injured casualty had fallen some 700 feet. Somehow he had survived. His headlong downward slide had been stopped at last, and he had found himself half-conscious and lying in the snow, the overhanging cornice now lost in cloud above him. His face was terribly bruised from the rough ground and his legs were strangely unwilling to obey him. In great pain he had managed to shuffle a little farther down the slope, and begun shouting for help. But who would still be on the mountain in such conditions? It seemed that after surviving such a fall, he must succumb to the appalling weather and die out there unable to crawl far enough to safety . . .

Not only the team on exercise were on their way off the hill, however, but also two more walkers, who had been fighting their way down through the white-out. Incredulous at first, they had heard the distant cries for help, faint against the howl of the storm, and somehow found their way to the casualty. One had set off as fast as he could to raise the alarm in the valley, while the other had volunteered to stay, wrapping the casualty in a bivvy sack and trying to keep him warm. The team found them together.

More team members were clawing their way up the mountain, often crouching for minutes at a time until the gale force gusts had passed. At last they located the third casualty of the afternoon. Although he had fallen a shorter distance, he was lying some 300 feet below the ridge, delirious and unaware of his surroundings. Both men had experienced potentially fatal falls, and their survival was a cause for wonder.

Conditions were so bad that the helicopter would not be able to fly in to evacuate the casualties, but Patterdale team had responded speedily to the emergency call. It would involve struggling through terrible conditions with stretchers from the valley below, but they were a highly experienced team, one of the busiest in the Lake District. They could be relied upon to be up on the mountain in record time. In the meantime, there was nothing to do but wait, and try somehow to protect the casualties from the extreme cold and deal with the injuries with what equipment they had available . . .

The team members huddled against the casualties, trying to keep them warm. All available gear had been emptied out of rucksacks and wrapped round them, insulating them against the cold of the ground. One of the members there was a First Aid specialist, and with other MRT members he was able to dress the wounds from the First Aid pack always carried even on exercise. Darkness was falling fast. The wind, even here, in as sheltered a spot as they had been able to find, battered them viciously. As they lay on the steep slope, every once in a while a particularly strong gust would send the whole party sliding farther down the icy fellside. The team members who were on the higher slope had been busy digging shelves and ledges for the stretcher when it arrived, and as it was too steep to lie down anywhere, they needed a place where they might huddle against the elements.

Everyone was exhausted and cold when at last the welcome lights of the Patterdale team appeared out of the gloom. Somehow they had managed to keep the casualties stable and comforted, and several times during their wait for help they had reflected on how lucky it was that they had chosen this spot, on this day, for a snowcraft exercise. Any one of the walkers so suddenly trapped by the freak conditions could have become a fatality very quickly if no one had been able to raise the alarm . . .

It was a long, long carry-down, in darkness, gale force winds and snow. Even for experienced MRT members it was a night none of them would ever forget.

The Land-Rovers, one now being driven by John Brown, had struggled up the fellside track, but they were unable to get as far as the teams, so the casualties had to be carried down to the hostel. By now the teams themselves were becoming seriously cold and exhausted. Injured casualties, and eventually half-frozen team members, were brought off the hill. A Land-Rover got stuck in the snow. The weather grew worse. Everyone was white with snow from head to foot, but they kept going until all casualties could be evacuated. Somehow ambulances, including the special four-track vehicle kept at Penrith hospital for heavy snow conditions, had managed to get through to the doctor's surgery, and now the injured could be quickly transferred to hospital.

But for the exhausted members of the local team the night was not yet over. A car had been found in the valley where it must have been since the morning. Another search was under way . . .

*   *   *

By Monday morning conditions had worsened, although that hardly seemed possible. In the early hours, an emergency summons came from the Kirkstone Pass between the two lakes, which was officially blocked by snow. Two families had been stranded the night before, and had spent the night in the local pub. An SOS was sent down to the police station, for they had run out of baby food, nappies, and medicine, and one of the children had a chest infection.

A trip to the chemist by the team leader, to buy supplies, was followed by a struggle up the pass in a Land-Rover. The families were distressed and worried. How long would the snow last? The problem was solved by taking them down to the police station, from where the roads had at least been temporarily cleared.

But warnings were sent out: snow was still falling, the winds were getting up, and however hard the snow ploughs worked, by evening the roads would be blocked again . . .

*   *   *

The phone was ringing and ringing . . . Dave, deep in exhausted sleep, struggled to wake up. It was Malcolm Grindrod . . . a SARDA call-out. Another search was on—a big one, with no real clue to the location of the missing walker. The Patterdale team had been out all night searching, and the dogs were to be called in as reinforcements. Conditions were terrible up on the fell, visibility nil . . . Dave came off the phone and, parting the curtains, looked out of the window onto the deserted street. Snow lay thick in the front garden and on the house tops and there was hardly any wind, but he knew from experience that such deceptive calm meant nothing. It could be blizzard conditions a mile or two down the road . . .

With Loch in the back of the car he drove as fast as he

dared down to Langdale/Ambleside base. It was already busy with team dogs piling into a Land-Rover. Loch jumped into the rear of the vehicle and sat, tail wagging, looking expectant. It was beginning to snow again and the wind was getting up. An RAF helicopter from Boulmer was coming to pick them up from the local rugby field; they were to get there as soon as possible. From there they would be taken to Patterdale base for a briefing and thence up into the fells. It would all save time and increase their effectiveness.

They ran in, crouching against the downdraught, and within seconds were taking off, the aircraft swinging against the wind. Dave looked down and saw the fellside below him. It was almost invisible behind a veil of snow, and as he watched it disappeared entirely in a white blanket. They clawed their way, lurching and bumping as the wind hit them, up onto the Kirkstone Pass; the pilot by this time must be flying on instruments alone. Outside the windows there was nothing but grey mist, broken by huge flakes of snow which skidded across the glass and were flicked away instantaneously. Dave felt the aircraft begin to lose height. They must be coming down into the valley on the far side. Once again the wind buffeted them, causing the tail of the helicopter to swing in the wind. A good thing he didn't get airsick. As always, his respect for the pilot grew by the minute. He had been on so many flights. There had been good ones and bad; sometimes, like today, the weather defied description. But always there was that same skill and dedication. You knew you were in the best hands . . .

They landed in the field on the far side of the pass and, with their dogs, piled into the team HQ for a briefing on their search areas. The lost walker had apparently set off the day before, and since then conditions had deteriorated very fast. By now the hill was highly dangerous. They would be flown up into an area between two coves, high on the face of the mountain, Dave Riley with Loch, Malcolm Grindrod with Mist and Spin, and Carol McNeill with Kimm.

Another bumpy flight, climbing up into the blizzard with their stomachs left behind somewhere on the school field. There were no gaps in the cloud now, and the wind was a wild animal, outraged to have its territory invaded. Eventually they made it to a ridge between the two coves. One by one they jumped out of the helicopter, which could do no more than hover above the mountain. It was a blind jump, with the downdraught from the rotors lifting the top snow into a blizzard of its own. Then that last friendly contact with the outside world vanished into the swirling mist, away down into the valley again.

They were left alone, crouched against the force of the wind as they tried to work their way down off the exposed ridge into the waist-high snow in the coomb, Malcolm Grindrod working in the middle and the other two on either side. It was a terrible place to be. The wind at this height was lethal, and to walk into it required a massive effort of will. Bent double in order to avoid being blown over, they felt as though they were pushing through a solid wall. They needed all their wits about them not to be swept off the crag into the unimaginable depths below. And all around them the snow was avalanching down the mountainside, small falls as yet, but a warning of what might be to come.

Occasionally the wind would die away, and they would be left, trudging through, sometimes at waist height, in an eerie quiet. As the blizzard eased, the great peaks would come into view, shrouded in an impenetrable secrecy and silence. Then the wind and snow would descend on them again, leaving them breathless, clogging up their snow goggles as fast as they cleared them. The dogs battled their way through, all three collies light enough not to get buried, doing their job.

Suddenly Loch took off, her body registering excitement. Snatched across the wind was the sound of frantic barking. Had she found? Dave walked on, waiting to see what she would do next. If she had picked up a scent she would be back, indicating positively . . .

The next second the world was turned upside-down. The wind almost knocked him flying and a white-out, snow travelling horizontally across the mountain straight in his face, cut out all vision. He no longer knew which was up and which was down. He stood still, bracing himself against the force of the wind, trying to breathe in the clogging stuff. It was like being buried alive. It might have lasted for seconds or minutes or forever—he had no sense of time. But when at last the wind slackened to only gale force and the snow eased a little, Loch was nowhere to be seen . . .

Dave tried not to be unduly worried. They had been in many white-outs together, and she was a strong, experienced dog, using to ranging well away from her handler. In a few minutes she would be back . . .

'Loch! Loch! Here, girl!'

The wind died away altogether for a few seconds and the cloud shifted enough for limited visibility. The snow stretched on upwards, his own footprints already blurred by the fierce gale and the new snow. But Loch was nowhere. He called and whistled again, listening intently for the sound of her bell collar. Nothing. Perhaps she was expecting him to follow her. The wind struck again, and once more he was doubled over against its force, the snow lashing at his face like a cat o' nine tails . . . Again he shouted into the wind. Nothing.

If he started walking, Loch, who must be higher up, would follow as she had so often done before . . .

He began to struggle down the mountain, wondering now whether he had left it too late. The weather was worse than he could ever remember, it must be gusting sixty, seventy miles an hour, perhaps more. He could no longer see the peaks, even in the pauses in the storm. It was like being in a white coffin which moved with you and threw you about so that you could hardly stand, which sapped your senses and your ability to think. The storm, you felt, wanted you for the mountain, and it wasn't going to let go that easily . . .

At last, after what seemed like hours of struggling waist high in snow, still calling against the wind, he made it to a farm in the valley, itself shrouded in snow and almost cut off. Dave trudged through the gate. Other team members, whitened, half-frozen ghosts, were waiting in the yard. Penny Melville was nursing a cut hand. She and Dave Brown, with Ian Wallace and Chris Francis, had experienced terrible freak winds in the cove area they were searching. Penny and her dog Ben had been lifted off their feet and flung bodily into a stone wall. Chris Francis' labrador Tarn had been thrown two hundred feet down the mountainside, while Chris had also experienced the terrifying sensation of being picked up by the wind like a stray leaf—despite his ice axe which he had buried deep into the snow—and hurled bodily across the steep face of the mountain. Only a last frantic jab with his axe had stopped him falling uncontrollably into the gully below. Everyone agreed that these were the worst conditions they had ever experienced. It was a sobering reminder of just how bad it could get . . . They were lucky to be down in one piece, but there was one member of the team who was still up there, in all that . . .

'I've lost my dog!' Dave shouted hoarsely above the screaming wind. 'I'll have to come back in the morning.'

'Surely she'll never survive up there?' A team member gestured up the hill, shaking his head.

'She's a tough little dog. She can survive anything! We've been through as bad as this before, though I'm not sure I can remember when!' Dave was trying to make light of it, trying not to think she might be lost, up there . . . 'She must just have got disorientated. The helicopter flight, perhaps. I'll get her in the morning. I'm sure she'll make it.'

These collies were tough as old boots, for all their fragile appearance. And Loch, who had been so much with him, was no exception. She knew how to find shelter, how to get out of the snow. He had confidence in her. He was sure in the morning he would find her safe and well . . .

*   *   *

As Dave was struggling down the mountain with his companions, the rest of the searchers were being called off the hill. Conditions had become impossible and it was no longer viable to risk the lives of the teams. It was in these white-out conditions that they came upon the lost walker. With unimaginable courage he had managed somehow to stay alive, but it had been a terrible night and a terrible day, one of the worst the fells had ever seen, and injury and cold were to prove too much. In the end this was one life they would not be able to save from the mountain . . .

9

'LOCH'S MISSING'

And now after the trauma of the last few days, Loch was lost on the mountain, in conditions which had already claimed lives in the last few terrible hours. Dave, coming home at last, weary and dispirited, had to tell Sheila and the family. It was very hard. He tried not to worry, but suddenly, it was as though someone had taken away his right arm . . .

Charlotte was really too young to understand, but picking up the phrase, kept repeating over and over, 'Loch's missing. Loch's missing.'

The house seemed empty without her. He was on duty the next night, but at first light, whatever the weather, he would try to get back up the mountain, even if he had to go alone . . .

All night he could hear the wind howling round the house. Even here, in the middle of the town. He slept lightly, too tired after the events of the last days, and too worried, to fall into a deep slumber. The morning light came sullenly into the room. The wind seemed to have abated, but outside the window every tree and wall and lamp-post had its deep covering of snow.

Malcolm Grindrod had volunteered to come with him, with his two graded Search Dogs, Mist and Spin. After all, they had worked together for years and trusted each other, both with years of experience on the mountain. Malcolm was the ex-training officer for SARDA, and one of two deputy leaders of Langdale/Ambleside team. And he had been there, the day before . . . he too had spent the night worrying about Loch . . . Stewart Hulse, Dave's team leader, had promised help with the search, as had Tom Fynn, team leader in Patterdale, and they were able to take a team vehicle up to the base of the fell.

Already offers of help were flooding in. Patterdale team were co-ordinating plans for a search. But for today, Dave and Malcolm would go up alone with Malcolm's dogs. Dave was confident that he only had to get up to the point, in Ruthwaite Cove, where he had lost contact with Loch, to find her waiting for him. It was just a matter of getting back up there.

But, although the snow seemed to lie tamed in the town, the fury of the storm spent at last, on the fellside it was wilder than he could ever remember in all his years in Mountain Rescue—even worse, if that were possible, than the day before. The wind was gusting almost to hurricane force, whipping up the snow into spindrift. It was like ploughing through thick, freezing, glutinous spray which smoked up out of the drifts and gullies like an evil genie. Sleet, travelling along the fellside in a horizontal path, hit them in the face with a physical force. They could hear the sinister roar of snow avalanching down the mountainside on either side of them. So much snow had fallen in the last few days. Apart from being blown off the mountain, being buried in an avalanche was a very real danger. The sleeping giant had woken and was showing his teeth. This was the wildest place in England, and the most savage. It could, with no exaggeration, have been the Arctic. In some senses it was more dangerous. It was what you sensed up here on a sweet, heather-scented summer's day—that this was an untamed place, and always would be; that it had nothing to do with civilisation, and that this wildness could kill you without even noticing. It was what you grew to love about the mountains, but it was what you pitted yourself against, and it was what could break you in the end.

And somewhere up there, in those frightful conditions, a small dog was lost and alone. The thought gave a spur to the two of them. If they could just make it to Ruthwaite Cove, Dave thought, she would be there, she would certainly be there. Even if (as he secretly dreaded) she was lying somewhere injured, then she wouldn't be far away, and maybe they could find her before it was too late.

They battled on, two whitened figures waist-deep in powder snow, half-frozen with cold, the sweat freezing on them, breath smoking in the air. It was so cold you could hardly breathe. Dave, pausing to take off his glove, found his hand had lost all feeling. It must be 40 below, with the wind-chill factor. Could any creature survive?

The wind was increasing to a pitch of hysteria when ahead of them they saw the outline of a bothy perched high on the fellside, on the opposite track, half-buried in snow. Incredibly, a figure clad only in a gaberdine mackintosh and a flat cap, bent over against the wind, was struggling up the fellside with a hay bale, trying to reach his sheep which were sheltering in the lee of the bothy.

Malcolm made his way across the gully towards the figure while Dave carried on, whistling with all his might against the storm.

'We've lost a collie!' Malcolm screamed across the wind. 'Black and white. Have you seen her?'

The figure stared back at him. The mackintosh was caked with snow and there was a fair covering on the cap, but otherwise the shepherd seemed unscathed by the fury let loose around him. He pushed the cap back on this head, looking puzzled.

'Have you seen a dog . . . lost . . . a lost collie?' It was almost impossible to make himself heard.

'I haven't seen owt!' The shepherd screamed back. 'But happen it'll coom down te farm. I'll keep me eyes skinned like, and tell the farmer. That'll need to be a tough owd bugger to survive this. It's a la'al bit snerpy terday!'

In just a few seconds of standing still, Malcolm was

numbed with cold. He shouted his thanks, and fought his way back to Dave on the far side.

'No luck! But I'll tell you something. They're a tough lot up here!'

They adjusted their snow goggles, set their faces into the driving snow, and struggled on, the two dogs following in their footsteps.

But it was hopeless. Gusts of wind were threatening to blow them off their feet. They could make no progress against it at all. For long seconds together they could only crouch against the snow, until the fierce gust had abated a little and they could take a few more tentative steps upwards. They began to realise there was no way they could get up the fellside to Ruthwaite Cove. The conditions were just too treacherous, and even if they could have gone on, it would have foolishly risked other lives than their own.

With heavy hearts they turned and began the long, exhausting fight back down the fell. Dave was still convinced that Loch would be up there, above them, sheltering close to the place where they had become separated, and so long as she wasn't injured, she would survive anything the mountain could throw at her. After all, the Herdwick sheep had been known to survive for three weeks in a snow drift, eating their own wool to keep alive. Loch might not be a sheep, but she had many of the same instincts of those hardy hill breeds, and was much more intelligent, and very experienced. He tried not to worry.

Loch was lost. And suddenly everyone knew. The television news and the national newspapers had got hold of the story. It had caught the public imagination, especially as Loch had been seen only a few weeks previously winning the PRO-Dog Gold Medal. On the PRO-Dog stall at Crufts that year, a picture of Loch was posted, with a daily bulletin, to cope with all the enquiries as to whether she had yet been found. She was the heroine of El Salvador, a plucky little dog, and dog lovers all over the country were rooting for her. But how long, realistically, could she survive in these extreme conditions? Three, four days? The guessing games began—except that it wasn't a game. The tables had been turned on this little dog who had helped to save so many lives on the mountain. Now she was dependent on others, in a race against time, to save her. If indeed she was still alive . . . No one could say.

Dave Riley was on shift that night. He spent the evening before he went to work telephoning round to all the farms in the area, putting them in the picture. If any of them should see a small black and white collie with a distinctive bell collar, they would know what to do. And the next day he was determined to try again.

Wednesday dawned bright and clear. The wind had died down to only gale force, but it was very, very cold. Dave had been touched by the response from well-wishers. Everyone wanted to help. John Brown had telephoned and said he was going to take a day's holiday from work and go out with some Penrith team mates, whatever happened. Patterdale team would be on hand to give support and organisation. Bill Pattinson was bringing across a group from Wasdale team. SARDA members had rung from as far away as Wales, including Dave Jones who had been with him in El Salvador. Neil Powell had telephoned from the Mountains of Mourne, offering to come over and give a hand. They all wanted to be there, knowing how it must feel, to lose your dog.

John Brown and some of the team members had a rendezvous at Patterdale Youth Hostel, where Joe Boothroyd, a team member, was the Warden. John had brought Sam and Tyan with him, and together with Richard Robinson from the team and other searchers, they decided to split initially into two parties and make their way up into Nethermost Cove and Ruthwaite Cove respectively. Dave was determined to get up as far as he had been before, higher if possible. John and the two dogs went with

Richard, while Tony Burton and Dave set off with another party to retrace his original route. Somewhere up there, he still believed, he would find the dog safe and well.

It was desperately cold, the snow whipped into fantastic shapes by the wind, too cold now for the dangers of avalanches. There were great drifts and snow fields blinding white in the sun, waves of shining snow like Dream Topping hanging against an intermittently blue sky. As Dave punched on up the hill, he stopped for breath occasionally and looked back, marvelling at the change from the wildness of the last few days. It was so often like that in the fells: savage weather when you couldn't feel anything but despair and even irrational anger against the elements which seemed to be trying so personally to destroy whatever dared to be on the mountain, and then, suddenly, pure, breathtaking beauty, sun on snow, great peaks marching away, a rose-coloured morning. It was like trying to love some fickle creature who turned you upside-down with her tantrums and her moods, and now, in these moments, showed her stunning beauty.

If he hadn't been so preoccupied he would have appreciated the glory of the mountains, laid out like the bare white bones of the world over the lake. It was very quiet, only the sound of the wind moaning over the desolation. There were no birds flying, no sounds of ravens; only the distant bleating of the penned sheep in the intake fields occasionally drifted up the mountain towards them.

They made it at last up to the snow field under High Crag, and split again into two parties, Dave straining his ears for any sound between shouts. The snow stretched away from them, unblemished, no sign now that they had ever walked that way. The blizzard and the wind had erased any memory of them. He could see now quite clearly right up to the summit of the crag. But there were no fresh paw marks, and no sound of barking, nor the distinctive sound of the bell collar which he would have been able to hear at least a quarter of a mile away. Nothing.

They climbed higher, to the point on the snow where Loch had taken off in that dreadful blizzard. It seemed a long time ago. Could she really still be alive? He needed all his deep-seated faith in his dog to make him believe it.

But the snow field was empty. Their voices rang around the crag, emphasising the emptiness.

'Loch! Loch! Here, girl!'

Nothing.

Patterdale Base was manning the radio, and at last they reported back that they were coming down. By now the sun had gone in and the wind had whipped itself up once more into a gale: it was bone-chillingly, numbingly cold. They met at the base of the fell in a dispirited group. They had all had the same experience: nothing, no clues, no distant sounds of barking. Just the emptiness of the frozen fellside.

'Thanks, everyone, for all you've done. I can't tell you how much I appreciate it. I just wish we could have had more success. But we'll try again tomorrow. Now we know she isn't up above Ruthwaite Cove we'll have to widen the search area.'

A reporter from the *Daily Mail* had arrived to see for himself. They had run the story from the beginning, and were as anxious as anyone to see a happy conclusion, although the odds were lengthening every day. The local papers and Border TV, BBC TV News, and the *Daily Express*, were all running stories of their own . . .

One set of people who knew Loch well had got wind of the search. The crews over at 'A' Flight RAF Boulmer had often carried the little collie and her master during Search and Rescue operations, even before the fateful day when she had become separated from him. An exercise was due to take place in the Lake District on the Thursday, and the Flight asked if they might be able to be of assistance in the search as part of the normal training operation. Looking for a small dog in snow was excellent practice for crews who were often required to carry out searches over vast areas of sea or difficult land terrain. They knew the value of

SARDA dogs in saving lives. If they could help out within their operational brief they would be very glad to do so.

Other volunteers, too, were arriving. It was snowing heavily in the Peak District, but that had not deterred John Tomlinson who had heard about Loch on the radio and immediately decided to set off and give a hand. With Steve Dowd and Malcolm Stirling from Derby MRT, they had set off at three o'clock that morning to fight their way over snow-covered roads into the Lake District, with John's Novice Search Dog Andy and Malcolm's Sam in the back of the Range-Rover.

They arrived just as dawn was breaking over the silent whiteness of the fells. The wind was howling across the valley, catching at them as they climbed wearily out of the vehicle. The snow was still falling in sharp, icy flurries. It was not going to be an easy day, and the forecast, although so much better than it had been for the last few days, was still pretty grim.

They were given an area from Striding Edge over towards Brown Cove and Glenridding Common, and Steve and John set off in deep snow up the Grisedale valley, the great black crags of Helvellyn lowering above them against the starkness of the snow.

As they were approaching Braesteads Farm, they saw to their astonishment a small black and white collie ahead of them, a dark blot against the landscape. It was running across the empty farmyard up towards the intake fields, and something about its panic-stricken flight made them realise that it was not a normal farm collie, but a dog in trouble.

John knew Loch well and when, in a lull in the wind, the sound of the bell collar came clearly across the snow, he pressed the button on his radio to give the news to base that the dog had been sighted.

Dave was travelling across the snowy Kirkstone Pass in the Land-Rover, the tyres slipping and sliding on the steep gradient. He was anxious to get back to the search. It was as though part of him was there, on the hill above Ruthwaite Cove, until he could get back and begin to call his dog again. Somehow he felt that this time, maybe, she would be there . . . Suddenly the radio in the vehicle crackled into life . . .

'Langdale Mobile One from Patrick Base . . . Positive sighting of Loch running in Braesteads Farm area. Please inform Dave Riley . . .'

Dave's feelings at that moment, overhearing the message on the Land-Rover radio, were an incredible mixture of incredulity, joy, and relief that his faith in Loch had been justified. What a dog! To survive the worst that the mountain could throw at her and still survive . . . he had never lost, somewhere deep down, a belief that she would still be alive, but somehow it still seemed incredible that she had come through those terrible days and nights on the fell and was still able to move about, apparently uninjured. Affection welled up inside him. She was a plucky little dog and he was proud of her. To have survived the worst storms for twenty years and still be running about—that was something close to a miracle.

But to the watchers the terrified movements of the dog were totally out of character. Loch had always been a great 'people' dog, ready to wag her tail and make a fuss of everyone, and this desperate flight up the fellside was not at all like her. They began to run towards her, calling out to her reassuringly as they did so. Loch redoubled her efforts to put as much distance between her and her pursuers as possible, eventually trying to squeeze through the slats of a farm gate to get out onto the open fellside.

The thought crossed John's mind that Loch would normally have jumped the intake wall without thinking about it and that she must be very weak.

They approached more cautiously, calling softly to her so as not to frighten her further. She had become entangled in the bars of the gate and was struggling desperately. But as they got closer she suddenly broke free and took off across the beck, swimming desperately against the torrent of meltwater, onto the far side and up the fellside like a train. She was heading up the southern side of the valley towards the summit known as Birks.

They decided to follow. If the weather clamped down again, they might never be lucky enough to sight her before she grew too weak to stand another onslaught of blizzard and cold. They reported their position to Patterdale Base and began to splash across the beck. It was very, very cold and very deep, the edges half-frozen and caked with snow. By the time they got to the far side, their boots were soaked. They started to climb. Loch had disappeared entirely into the tops. The wind was getting up; spindrift, whipped from the drifts, misted their vision. They would be lucky to get another sighting.

Two hours later, when they had almost given up hope, suddenly, out of the snowclouds, they glimpsed her again. By then they had made their way, laboriously, across from Birks, towards Grisedale Tarn, that dark, mysterious pool which had given birth to so many legends. They heard a dog bark, once, twice, and there above them was Loch on the skyline. She stood for a moment, as though uncertain, pulled by the scent of human beings, but still desperately afraid. John's Alsatian looked up, ears pricked, his head on one side. Then the small black and white shape disappeared into the mist.

By now a Sea King from RAF Boulmer, with Flt Lt Jan Warren as Pilot and Captain, Flt Lt Neighbour as co-pilot, Flt Lt Williamson as Winch Operator and Navigator, and Flt Sgt Turnbull as Winchman, were airborne and preparing to give assistance. It was good to be able to lend a hand, and everyone back at base was wishing them luck, hoping that today they would come up trumps. The Sea King landed in Patterdale and picked up Dave Riley so that he could help scrutinise the ground as they flew.

The media had turned up at Patterdale in force. There were television crews from local and national stations, and a number of national newspapers. They had all made the hazardous journey down to the team headquarters, hoping for a happy ending to the story. All across the country now people were rooting for Loch, hoping that she would be found alive.

'It's a big story, Dave,' One of the cameramen said as he set off. 'Don't forget to come back here if you find the dog. We must get a good picture. However tired you are, don't leave us in the lurch! And good luck!'

They had already made several passes over the valley when suddenly, they saw below them on Birkhouse Moor a frantically waving figure with a small dark shape beside it. The helicopter swooped in low. It was a walker. He had a collie beside him. The aircraft touched down and Dave jumped out, blinded again by the spindrift. The figure came towards him.

'I heard on the radio this morning you were searching for a collie,' the figure shouted across the wind. 'I think I've found it. It's been following me for hours. Obviously lost.'

Dave peered through the snow at the dog which was restrained on a piece of rope. It wasn't Loch, but another hopeful-looking black and white dog collie who was looking up at him, tail swishing on the snow.

'I'm afraid it isn't mine, but we'll take him with us,' he shouted. 'We might spot his owner on the way up. Thanks for your help!'

He took hold of the rope and began to run towards the waiting helicopter, fighting his way through the snow spray which the rotor blades were whipping up into a blizzard. He remembered as he ran how frightened the dogs usually were when they had to run in under the rotors. Loch hated that part. But this dog showed not a sign of fear, scrambling eagerly into the helicopter as though he had been doing it all his life, and settling under the seat like an old hand. He was obviously looking forward to the ride.

Dave gestured to the winchman, and then pressed his throat mike.

'It isn't Loch! Another lost collie!'

The winchman shook his head in disbelief. They swept up once more into the clear air above the snow.

Suddenly the pilot picked up the radio message from John who had spotted Loch again below Lord's Seat, and the helicopter, which had been flying low over the crag while Dave scrutinised the ground below for movement, banked and turned towards Grisedale Tarn. John was frantically scrambling up the fellside, calling for all he was worth. At one point the dog again appeared on the skyline, advanced tentatively towards them and then scrambled away over the snow with that same panic-stricken flight. It seemed hopeless. Loch must be so deranged by her dreadful ordeal that even her own sense of survival and her need for human beings were not enough to overcome this terrible fear. Would they ever be able to catch up with her in this vast wilderness, with the weather getting worse by the minute?

Suddenly Dave caught his first sight of Loch. She was running around on the path below them. The pilot too had seen her. Coming as low as he dared in the mist and snow, he hovered above the snow field. Dave stood in the open doorway, took a deep breath, and jumped. The snow was deep just there, and very cold. For a moment he was blinded by the snow flurry as the downdraught from the helicopter swept the powder snow into a blizzard around him. It was hard to get his breath, let alone his bearings. But then he saw her. She was making off up onto the tops again like a bat out of hell. The sound of the helicopter, which she had never liked at the best of times, was just too much.

'LOCH!' he bellowed. 'LOCH! Here, girl!'

But it was no use, She turned once, but he was downwind of her, and she had no scent. He must have looked to her a strange, terrifying figure, shrouded in spindrift. She began to run, vanishing once more in the direction of Birks. Dave began to run towards her, but even after four days without food, and after all she had been through, she was still one of the best, too fast for him. He stood in the snow, feeling helpless, as she disappeared.

John and Steve watched as Dave was picked up once more by the hovering helicopter. It was obvious that the noise of the engines was making things worse and driving Loch into more of a panic. There could be a danger that she might come off the crag, driven by fear, and yet . . . there seemed no other way of catching up with her.

The helicopter fell away above them into the crag. Obviously the pilot had decided the same thing. There would have to be a different strategy if they were to succeed.

'Can you get ahead of her?' Dave spoke into the throat mike. 'If you can drop me upwind of her and then fly away I might have a better chance.'

Suddenly they spotted her again. She was streaking across Gavel Moss towards Birks and Black Crag, a tiny spot in the white landscape. She seemed to be driven by some strange compulsion, running on and on.

'We'll drop you up ahead. Then get right away. Radio us if you need help. And good luck!'

They flew ahead of Loch, high up so that she wouldn't be frightened again by the engines. She stopped for a moment, one paw raised as they clattered over, then once again resumed her mindless galloping. The pilot was reminded of a dog he had once seen pounding down a country road, hopelessly lost, its paws raw with running, but driven somehow to go on and on . . .

Once more the helicopter hovered low over the frozen landscape, throwing up a tornado of powder snow. Dave took a deep breath and jumped down. Once again, as the helicopter clawed away and the wind slewed the spindrift around him, it was seconds before he could see where he was. It was snowing up here, too, and viciously cold.

But as the air cleared, he saw with a sinking heart that she had once again overtaken him and was even now disappearing fast through the snow flurries, over the horizon. In desperation, with every fibre of his being, he screamed into the wind.

'LOCH!'

She stopped, high up now on the crag. For a moment the snow blotted her out, and Dave's stomach turned over. But when he could see her again she was still there, looking back. He stood still, heart in mouth, and called again.

'LOCH! Here, girl! It's me, girl! Here, Loch!'

She began, warily, to retrace her steps, very slowly, until she was sideways on to him, still a fair distance away. The wind was blowing steadily at him, but as she moved round, suddenly she caught his scent. With years of communication between them he could read all her signals. Her ears went up. With everything in him he willed her to come back.

'Loch! It's me. Here, lass.'

For a moment she sat down in the snow, her head to one side, studying the wind, only twenty yards away now, but cautious, afraid.

'Good dog. Here, lass.'

Then, in a dramatic instant, she got the full scent of him. The effect was electric. She was suddenly streaking towards him across the snow. Still yards away, she took a flying leap into his arms, licking his face in an ecstasy of joy, whining deep in her throat. And he held her, feeling her heart-stopping thinness after all those days on the mountain, saying thank you . . .

The media were waiting for them, cameras poised. After all, he had promised. But Dave had a surprise for them as he leaped out of the helicopter: two dogs instead of one! It caused some consternation. Loch, with a cut paw and still afraid, had to be persuaded out from under the seat where she had hidden herself on the flight down, but the other mystery passenger was throughly enjoying being in the limelight. It wouldn't be long before his master caught up with him and had him back at work with his sheep on the fellside, but in the meantime, he was going to make the most of it!

'Lost for four days on the mountain in the worst weather for twenty years' . . . 'Loch is Safe' . . . 'Safe in the hands of the law!' and finally 'Loch back on duty' . . . Only four days later, Loch was called out to help in a search of old mine workings near Dalton-in-Furness. The cut paw had healed; Sheila was feeding her up. The Riley family were getting back to normal, despite a trip to Manchester for Dave and Loch to appear on BBC News the night of the rescue and letters pouring through the letter box. It was amazing and touching and heart-warming how many people cared, how many people had taken the trouble to write, to send donations for SARDA; how letters addressed to 'Loch, Helvellyn', and 'The Master of Loch, Windermere', dropped through the box courtesy of the Post Office. Loch's lonely fight out there on the fells had touched the hearts of thousands of people . . .

On the Friday I drove up to Cumbria for the Annual Course. I had been besieged in my own Sussex village by people stopping me—outside the shop, coming out of church—or ringing up: 'Any news? Has she been found? Surely she can't survive . . . ?' But she had, and here she was, tail wagging, licking my hand, with Dave in the car park. This year she would have her three-yearly reassessment, as Sam had the previous year. It didn't matter that a week before she had been half-buried on the mountain for four days, those were the rules. I put my hands around her middle. She was still thin. She wriggled and licked. The same old Loch. But would she be up to a rigorous reassessment after all . . . ?

On the Sunday of the course I stood in the valley below Dale Head and watched as Dave set Loch to work. It was a bright, sparkling day, the sun held in the cup of the valley like chilled wine, the tops snow-covered. Ravens cracked above us. It was impossible to imagine the hell of a week ago, it seemed as though it had never been . . . The assessors had their binoculars trained on the fellside, a vast area between the scree at the head of the valley and the beck. Together Dave and Loch made their way across the boggy ground at the base of the fell, and then we heard the command whistle as Dave sent Loch away, up into the crag. Suddenly she was off, streaking effortlessly over boulders, through bracken, light-footed on the loose shale, until she stood triumphantly above us all, looking down.

'Away, Loch. Away . . .' Obliquely, with that graceful movement of hers, she came across the fell, picking up the wind. No trace of tiredness, no fear. The sun shone on her out of a blue sky, benignly, and there was a snow wind cold enough to stir the blood. It was as though the fells themselves had forgotten they had tried to take her . . . But perhaps Loch herself would never forget . . .

10

VOICES OF SARDA

'It must be a handler. Who else would carry four leads, 150 feet of rope (for long searches) two dog bowls, two hundredweight of Choc-Drops, an assortment of whistles and a dog toilet. True, that description would fit most park keepers and councillors . . . but they don't paint red crosses on dogs' backs . . .' 'Kipp' Brown.

'What is it, I wonder, that is so attractive about training for years to wander the hills in the middle of another winter's night with one's friend and companion, the dog?' John Brown.

'Sometimes I feel it is not so much a man and his dog, but rather two animal species enjoying a special relationship and each other's company. But I think this has developed because of the work we have done together, and perhaps I am a bit of a sentimentalist and I'm imagining it all. People say dogs cannot reason but I am not sure. I think they can in a canine, limited way,' Ex-Handler.

We have just arrived on the Friday night for the PAL Annual Course, and everyone is busy renewing old friendships. To be invited to attend the four-day February course is the goal of every handler from the beginning. For this is the time when trainee SARDA dogs will hope to be promoted to Novice, which means they can at last be part of the call-out network, and Novice dog handlers can hope for the coveted full Search Dog status. And it is a time for meeting up, for planning the year ahead, and for seeing how the organisation, now so far-flung, is getting on . . . Dogs and handlers will travel the length of the country for training courses through the year, but for many graded dog handlers the PAL Annual Course in Keswick is the only time they really get together . . .

The entrance of the Crow Park Hotel is a sea of (as yet) clean boots and rucksacks. The usual banter is being shouted about in the corridors, insults and greetings between friends who may at any time be sharing difficulties and potential dangers . . .

'How do? How's that mangy, flea-bitten excuse for a search dog?'

'Have you seen the search areas on the map? I've got cramp already . . .'

'Crag? What crag? You won't catch me up there. I came here for a rest.'

'Don't tell me I have to share a room with you. I hope you brought a spare pair of socks this time . . . four days is too much, mate! I had a good mind to put in a complaint . . .'

'Anyway, we were right in the middle of the scree, and it was beginning to move, and I said, 'If I weren't a rock climber I'd be really scared and she said, "I AM a rock climber and I am really scared. Let's get out of here . . ."'

'Never again. I'll stick to the footpath next time. I'm too old for this sort of thing . . .'

Neil Powell has been travelling all day from County Down in Ireland with the ultimate rucksack (so heavy that no one else could lift it). They had all only just arrived and some were pretty tired. Phil Haigh had bidden a heartfelt farewell to his pupils for half-term, and had raced over at top speed after struggling to find his gear (one year, rumour has it, he forgot to take his dog) . . . the climbing shirt he always wore had been tracked down to the linen basket, a pair of boots, one without a lace because the kids had pinched it. The exuberance of finding the dog lead only to find the pup had chewed it up!

The following is a definitive list of gear for winter hill conditions, all of which must be brought for the course, and more importantly for a possible call-out:

Thermal T-shirt	Gloves
T-shirt	Balaclava
Thermal longjohns	Cagoule
Socks	Overtrousers
Breeches	Gaiters
Polar jacket	Boots

IN THE RUCKSACK

Carry mat	First Aid Kit
Survival tent	Medical Wipes
Spare blanket or	Torch battery, spare bulb
sleeping bag	Maps
Duvet jacket	Breeches compass and whistle
Emergency rations	Radio and battery
Food and drink	Dog whistle and lead
Ice axe	Dog rewards
Crampons	Dog coat
Goggles	Dog harness
Rope	Dog food
Net	Coolight

(Tin of Spaghetti Bolognese for morale boosting!)
Question: How do they ever get off the ground?

It was good to see old friends again. John Brown would be over later in the evening from his home. Sam was not up for reassessment—that had been the previous year—but John, as an experienced handler, was being asked to help assess the dogs over the next four days in a gruelling series of tests designed to weed out any potential weaknesses in a dog and handler team who would be, ultimately, vital links in a life-saving chain.

And it would in no way be a formality. I have a vivid memory of one dog, who had travelled hundreds of miles with his handler hoping for Novice grade, being sent home on the first morning, after the stock test had shown him as having a potential 'eye for the sheep', a fatal flaw in any Search Dog and one which SARDA can never afford to take on as a risk. Every year a proportion of handlers will fail, after two, maybe three years of dedicated training, day after day. And for a few, the disappointment will be too much and they will never return. It will be the end of a dream.

A series of maps have been put on the wall, describing the various areas we will be using and, alongside, the groupings the handlers will be in, and the areas to which the 'bodies' will be assigned. Some of the bodies, too, have travelled hundreds of miles to be here, just in order to lie out in snow and rain for six or seven hours a day for the next four days, and wait to be found by a dog. Mind you, it has its positive side. There are no telephones, with the right equipment they will be fairly warm (I have to say I have never managed to eliminate two or three cold spots including my nose, but then I am not an experienced veteran like some), and it is quite possible to go to sleep. However, it is not entirely a good idea to be lulled into a false sense of security, as you are likely at some stage to have your pleasant doze interrupted by a frantically excited dog who attempts to lick you clean (keep off the honey sandwiches) and deafen you at the same time. 'Kipp' Brown's wonderful article in the 1982 SARDA Report summed it up pretty well:

> Now bodying is fast becoming a dangerous occu-
> pation and not to be treated lightly. Deaths from
> boredom and sunstroke after six hours of not being
> found are not uncommon, and you run the risk of
> being licked to death . . . or totally disregarded (this
> usually happens when the same dog has found six times
> in 30 minutes). Having found you it disappears,
> presumably to indicate the same to its handler unless
> you are unlucky, in which case it returns and drops

half a tree in your lap. Its handler . . . is puffing and panting up the hillside, blowing his dog whistle like a demented railway guard . . .

The actual indication can be anything from carrying a car tyre in its mouth to cocking its leg at your wellies; you do get the odd one who just barks but we don't talk about them! He (the handler) then proceeds to chase the poor animal across the moor, waving his arms and screaming, 'SHOW ME! SHOW ME!' which not only frightens the tourists, but leaves a 'body' . . . to sit there and wait for 30lbs of smelly fur to land on top of him, barking in his ear and depositing the inevitable paw on his testimonials . . . (Sorry about that. Ed.)

(The handler) smiles contentedly at you as you sit there removing dog hairs from your cheese and tomato sandwiches, wishing you had stuck to the less hazardous occupation of blindfolded lion tamer . . .

It can be even more hazardous still, as the Irish handler Neil Powell recounts:

It was in March and the snow was deep, and for the most part, the dogs were the usual impeccably good-natured and well-mannered companions we all know so well. However, there was one exception—a very big, muscular brute whose variety I will not divulge . . .

The dog hated me from the first moment we met, and he jumped at every opportunity to display his inordinately large and well developed canines and incisors especially for me . . .

I had to keep suppressing a rising panic that threatened to break me down into a gibbering wreck. I had never seen a snow grave before, let alone been buried in one . . . It is about three feet deep, fits one exactly, and has at one end a small hollowed-out section to ensure an air supply. The 'body' is imprisoned and concealed from above by blocks of snow carefully levered into position . . . no movement is possible except wriggling of toes and fingers . . .

As the last block of snow was lowered onto me I remembered . . . a green squeaky toy hedgehog . . . what had the handler said to me?

'If Robert (the name has been changed to protect the innocent) starts anything(!!) when he finds you, give him the hedgehog and it will keep him busy until I arrive!'

With this memory to torment me . . . and the hedgehog belatedly remembered in an inaccessible trouser pocket . . . the sky vanished, and there I lay . . .

I had plenty of time to let my anxieties grow as for some reason 45 minutes ticked away, and I was just beginning to feel like cracking up when I heard the unmistakable sound of a dog snuffling closer. I experienced just for a moment the unbounded joy the avalanche victim feels when he knows he is about to be snatched from the jaws of death. But then the irony of it struck me when I realised that the exact opposite was about to happen—I was about three feet away from death's very eager jaws! . . . Then I remembered the hedgehog and began scrabbling and searching, trying to reach it . . . then the roof cracked and creaked and very slowly and deliberately an enormous black snout pushed through. He was already taking tentative nips at my anorak . . . Suddenly I found the hedgehog and with great skill manoeuvred it into his wide-open mouth . . .

He set about the hedgehog which squeaked and shrieked as it was demolished and shredded . . . At last, with milliseconds to spare, the handler arrived . . .

'Well done . . . nice bit of bodying, lad! But why the hell did you give him the . . . hedgehog? That's Robert's and he's still to come. . . !

*   *   *

We are all ranged along tables in the dining room of the Crow Park. The room, with its sepia pictures of old Cumbria, is a haven of peaceful charm for the rest of the year, but for these next four days it has been taken over by brightly coloured fleecy jackets and men and women in red socks (no boots allowed) and mountain rescue stories and a great deal of laughter. Perhaps it is the nature of the beast, but everyone laughs a lot. It's the same in the Mountain Rescue teams. An essential ingredient for when things get a bit tricky, an essential part of friendship and teamwork, is this wonderful sense of humour which is the first thing that strikes a newcomer. There is a tremendous atmosphere. David Langford, the owner of the Crow Park, a Keswick team member and an ex-dog handler, presides over it all with his wife. It's the upside of trudging about all day on a rain-swept scree slope, which may be what tomorrow will bring . . .

The stories are flying backwards and forwards. Next year, as I say to myself every year, I must go on a diet BEFORE I go on the course. Not only so that I can get into my best breeches without risking cutting myself in half, but so that I can eat the wonderful Crow Park Cumbrian cooking with a clear conscience. For some, however, this meal is likely to be their last for a while, and so will be particularly welcome . . .

It was on the final night of the Annual Course last year that there was a call-out, a search over Honister and the Newlands Pass for a missing boy. After an overnight search he was found safe near Red Pike by a Search Dog and handler. Now—would you believe it?—the call comes on the first night of the Annual Course, not the last. Which is worse?

The phone rings after dinner, in the middle of the Assessors' meeting . . . Phil Haigh is feeling drowsy after all those helpings. It has already been a long day . . .

'When marking a find try to assess . . . Pete, would you answer the phone?'

More telephone calls. People being asked out of the room . . . everyone is becoming a little restless . . . alarm bells are ringing in our heads. Dave carries on.

'If the dog doesn't range far . . .'

Pete comes back looking serious.

'Sorry, Dave, we've got a call-out . . . at Ennerdale. Ian's gone off to Cockermouth Base to see Jim and sort out deployment of dogs. We've decided to send ten dogs initially to assist.'

By now Pete has the undivided attention of the whole group. No witty comments, no disruption, just intently listening to every word. We all sit waiting to hear who the ten dogs will be . . .

'Neil Powell, John Brown, Phil Haigh . . .' Senses suddenly heighten with the onset of a tang of excitement and anticipation that always accompanies a call-out. It disappears five minutes after you've started but it's quite nice for a while . . .

In a phenomenally short time the handlers have gone, their rucksacks packed, emergency food and a hot drink if they are lucky, dogs retrieved from the backs of cars, hardly able to believe their good fortune, warm gear hastily put on or grabbed from the boot . . . It suddenly seems very quiet, as though all the action is elsewhere, which indeed it is . . . We hear about it later.

*   *   *

They arrived at the Cockermouth Base and filed into the briefing room. Jim Coyle gave a thorough briefing on the missing people . . .

'Four lads, walking in the Red Pike area. The two slightly more experienced apparently decided to come back by the longer route. They separated in the Ennerdale valley, about here . . .' Jim pointed to the map . . .' They were going to meet up in the pub for a meal. By nine o'clock, when the other two hadn't shown up, their mates were getting pretty worried. It had started snowing . . . anyway, they decided to contact us from the pub . . .'

Jim had been bleeped as usual by the police after the 999 call and had made his way down to Cockermouth Base. The team had been called out, and Jim had phoned through to the Crow Park Hotel, contacting SARDA, and asking for dogs . . .

'As far as we know their experience is limited and they don't have bivvying gear. Conditions are quite hazardous. There is new snow, and there is a definite danger of avalanche. These are your search areas . . .'

The two main dogs would be on Pillar, searching the Ennerdale side of Pillar Rock to the summit, taking in the various climbing areas in case they had fallen. There would be Cockermouth team members assigned to them who were experienced in the difficult terrain. One dog would take out the west flank and the other would take a traverse used by climbers across the front of Pillar . . . John Brown and Sam, with two other handlers, were given the area of Scarth Gap across to Green Gable.

Phil Haigh and his collie Tosh, with Martin from Cockermouth team, and Chris Francis and his yellow labrador Tarn, also with a guide from Cockermouth, had been assigned to Pillar, where the snow was already in a treacherous state. The problem was that the evening was very warm and there were large areas of instability, with the attendant threat of avalanche. Having got their kit together they transferred to the Cockermouth Land-Rover and sped off towards Ennerdale.

Slowly they ascended the steep, rough track until they came to some rocky outcrops where, due to the temperature, they elected to take off some of the outer clothing they were wearing. It was an extremely warm night and the hill fog was quite thick, giving only some twenty yards visibility . . .

'Cockermouth Relay from Search Dog Phil, do you read? Over.'

'Search Dog Phil, go ahead . . .'

'Cockermouth Relay, Search Dogs Phil and Chris are now separating to search the west flank to the summit and the traverse across Pillar Rock . . . Over.'

'Message understood. What are the conditions like? Over.'

'Very mild and thick hill fog. We have not reached the snow line as yet. Visibility 20-30 yards. Over.'

'Thank you for that. Listening out.'

Other messages were beginning to flash across the radio. It was now obvious that all the dog parties were deployed on the hill. The search was in full swing. A one-sided conversation between Base and Mobile would go on for the length of the operation—who had searched what, the clearing of areas, which Search Dogs were where, and were they OK?

As Phil and Martin shone their torches in the distance to locate the track, the mist seemed to be thinning. They could only hope that it would continue. It would help them enormously in their attempts to pick out a route in such difficult conditions. By now they were on a steep scree slope, traversing upwards towards a group of rocks with a thin rock rib running away up and to the right. Tosh, Phil's dog, was finding it hard going as she went across, nose in the air, quartering the ground. It was a lethal mixture of scree and water, and every time the dog attempted to get through, she would begin to slide back down . . .

'Away up, lass, Find, girl.'

Encouraged by the voice of her master, Tosh tried again. It was very frustrating, Every time she made a bit of height, she would lose some of it again by sliding downwards. It made her progress very slow. Her tongue hung out of the side of her mouth, and she was panting with the exertion. But she is a tough little collie. Somehow she just kept plodding on upwards.

At last they spotted more stable ground, which proved to be the rock rib. Martin led the way up. Phil was struggling, and cursing the fact that he had only a few days before modified his head torch to fit his caving helmet for his work in Cave Rescue. Why was it, when you needed something it was always somewhere else? To juggle a hand torch and climb at the same time was not easy. Every time Phil let go of the torch in order to use his hands it would end up pointing in the wrong direction.

Eventually they came to the snow line. There was a big area of snow they would have to traverse to take them up onto Pisgah Buttress. From there they would ascend to the top of Pillar via a gully on the right-hand side. It was the beginning of the serious climbing.

They stopped and took out their ice axes. Both men knew how tricky the snow was in these conditions. The slightest slip might set off an avalanche, not only risking their lives but also the lives of the searchers below them. They put on their gloves and jackets.

'See you at the bottom,' one of them joked, dissipating the tension with the usual black humour.

'Yes, it looks like fun.'

They began climbing, Martin in the lead, sinking up to his thighs in deep, wet snow. Phil followed on behind, sending Tosh away across the slope. It was even worse for her. She was a small dog, and the snow was too soft for her to run over the top as she would normally do. Her legs kept breaking through, but it was so deep they couldn't reach bottom, so she was left to thrash about on nothing. Phil saw her difficulties and waded across to her, half-lifting, half-pushing her onto firmer ground. She rewarded him with a lick.

'Search Dog Phil from Cockermouth Relay. Over.'

'Go ahead, Relay.'

'What is your position? Over.'

'Wait five until we get off this snow field. Over.'

'Roger to that.'

It was not the best moment to have a conversation. The snow was in an extremely poor state, very dangerous. They would be lucky to get off it. Very slowly and carefully they made their way across to the other side, conscious that one false movement could be enough to set the whole lot cascading down the mountain . . .

They radioed back their position to the Relay, together with a description of the conditions which had been requested by the team leader . . .

'The mist is clearing, visibility good but still very mild. The snow is deep and wet. It looks and feels very unstable.'

They discussed their position. Phil was grateful for Martin's special knowledge of Pillar. He was an expert climber, and this was his patch. Where handlers would normally be working on their own, it was because the conditions were so dangerous that they had of necessity been assigned a 'guide' climber of a high standard who was very familiar with the geography of the Pillar.

'If we climb up the gully we can check the top of the Shamrock traverse and see whether anyone has come to grief.'

Martin set off again, through the deep wet snow which had the consistency of sugar. Phil followed. Suddenly the snow gave way and they sank up to their chests. For a split second it seemed as though they had been caught in an avalanche, but the snow settled down again. Tosh struggled on ahead into the deep gully, knowing what was expected of her. They could see the strange incandescent glow of her coolight bobbing and weaving in mid-air as she fought her way to the top. She was a brave little dog. There wasn't much that would defeat her.

Then at last she had made it. She turned round triumphantly, twin stars shining back at them as the torch was reflected in her eyes. They struggled on after her, and a few moments later, apprehension forgotten, they were looking out over a magical landscape. Peak after peak marched in silence away into the distance of the night, their slopes silvered by the moon. The mist had cleared on the tops, and the mountains were etched into the star-filled night. All around them was a great sense of peace under the glowing stars. It was moments like these which made it all worth while, made all the discomfort and danger almost an irrelevance, certainly forgotten. Phil remembered Mallory's words when asked why he had wanted to climb Everest: 'Because it's there.' To someone who loves mountains, that says it all . . .

Messages were coming over the radio which made it clear that Base were growing increasingly concerned about the danger of an avalanche. Chris was working several hundred feet below Phil and Martin, and he was particularly dependent on the party above not setting off a fall of snow which might start a major avalanche. In warm, muggy conditions the top snow can rapidly become unstable, and with the smallest of catalysts, it can begin to shift alarmingly on the ice beneath until its accumulated weight causes tons of snow to roar down the mountainside like an express train, burying everything beneath.

Phil felt the responsibility of working Tosh in such a way that the risk of starting an avalanche was minimised. There was also the ever-present fear that she might suddenly disappear over the edge. Several years before, three Search Dogs had fallen 300 feet on Helvellyn onto the boulders just above Red Tarn. They had been working just in front of the handlers in a white-out when the first two dogs disappeared. The third, losing its grip, turned and barked at its handler before disappearing into the darkness below. And then there had been Sam's dramatic plunge over the crag which he had so miraculously survived. For every handler that was almost the biggest fear—that his dog, feeling its way ahead on a snow-covered mountainside, in a blizzard or in poor visibility particularly, might suddenly disappear, sometimes having fallen hundreds of feet through a cornice.

It was something you always held in your mind, but you

couldn't let it get in the way of your judgement. If there
were difficult places where the dog must work in order to
help save lives, then it had to happen that way. But there
were dogs who never came back . . .

At last they found themselves climbing across the snow-
covered scree which led to the summit of Pillar. Tosh,
relieved to be near the top, and feeling the ground
flattening out towards the summit plateau, galloped off,
quartering the ground enthusiastically. Suddenly, ahead of
them in the torchlight, was the summit cairn—the pile of
stones which traditionally marks the highest point of the
mountain, and which is added to by almost every walker
who feels that same sense of achievement in getting there.

'Cockermouth Base from Dog Phil. We are at the summit
of Pillar, taking 15 minutes' rest. Over . . .'

Tosh came and set beside them expectantly as they
opened their rucksacks. She had worked hard, and as a
valued member of the party, felt that a meal break was in
order for her, too. Phil lovingly unwrapped the Mars Bar
he had been thinking about all night as they struggled
through the waist-high snow. It was just what he needed!
Tosh, leaning equally lovingly over his shoulder, demolished
it in one gulp. It seemed unfair to protest. Instead he made
do with a revolting cup of coffee which tasted as though it
had been stewed for several days in old walking boots.

They leaned back against the cairn, tiredness kept at bay
by the pleasure of being there, on the summit, on a clear
night with snow on the mountain. In the distance they
could see the dull orange glow of Whitehaven, but to the two
searchers, in space and time it might have been on another
planet.

To misquote a famous line, the hills by now were
alive with the sound of radio messages flashing backwards
and forwards between Base and the Relay and the
searchers on the hill. It was time to go on. Phil repacked his
rucksack and they began to make their way down onto the
head of the corries which fell away steeply from the

summit. This was an area which was corniced heavily, the walls of snow standing out from the edge of the crag with deceptive solidity. They had already seen and marked them from below on the way up, but from above they looked even more lethal. Heavy tongues of snow stuck out into space, defying gravity, incised with deep cracks which marked their eventual downfall into the depths below.

In view of the conditions it would have been suicidal to venture too far onto such dangerous ground. Carefully, heart in mouth, the two searchers and the dog moved around the lip, trying with their torches to spot any breakthrough, any debris which might suggest a fallen body below them. These were tricky moments when any slip or sudden movement might send those immense walls of snow crashing down onto the search parties beneath.

Suddenly Tosh took off, bounding across the snow in that determined way she always displayed when she had picked up a scent.

'Has she got something, Phil?'

Phil was concentrating too hard to answer. He began to move faster across the hill. Tosh turned left towards the head of the corrie, her coolight weaving across the snow, reflecting greenly around her. Phil's stomach contracted. What if she went over? But to his immense relief she stopped and turned. A pause and she began to run towards him . . .

'Good girl, Tosh! Show me! Show me!'

She ran straight back to the edge and stood there with her nose pointing down the gully. Phil turned to shout as loud as he dared.

'I think she's got something, Martin, but I'm not sure what it is . . .'

Martin made his way as quickly as he could across the snow, but as he did so Phil caught a brief flash of torchlight somewhere below him. He pressed the button on his radio . . .

It was Chris, working Tarn several hundred feet below.

But it wasn't his scent that Tosh was picking up, he was sure of that. After a few moments, the truth dawned. Below Chris, struggling through the snow conditions on the lower slopes of the mountain, far, far below, the back-up team were toiling up the mountainside. Tosh, with her acute nose, had picked up their scent . . .

The adrenalin ebbed away. For a moment he had been sure. It was always a disappointment, after a long night's searching. But Tosh had done her job and done it well. And that in itself was heartening. Her senses were as sharp as when they had started so many long hours before.

'Good dog! Good dog, Tosh. You're a clever girl.'

They worked on in the dark. It would be dawn soon, and there was that particular kind of cold you get on the mountain just before the sun rises, when everyone is very, very tired.

Half an hour later they met up again with Chris and his companion. They too had had a difficult time in the deep snow. Chris and Phil paired up again and continued to work the hill, making their way down towards Black Sail Pass. There was a brief moment when they had to be put back on the path by the two 'guides', after losing their way. As they were just about to start an accidental ascent of Kirk Fell in the dark, they were very grateful but somewhat embarrassed! It was so easy to get disorientated, but they would undoubtedly pay for it later!

At last they were looking down into Ennerdale, just as dawn was beginning to appear behind the mountain tops in streaks of red and grey. Far, far below them they could see the welcome sight of the Land-Rover's flashing light. They began the steep descent, still working the dogs. Behind them, flickering lights lit up the top of the pass in an eerie way as the search parties, too, began their descent. They had safely negotiated the snow fields and could now begin the tiring walk down to the Youth Hostel below.

Forty minutes later and they were all together, the jokes and the black humour, the suffering of some poor

unfortunate who had been caught out with two left feet
. . . next time it would be someone else. It was a necessary
antidote to those long, long hours of difficulty and danger
when you were so very alone . . .

An hour's wait, to see whether the missing people might
walk off the hill at dawn. It happens so often, after
someone has been able to bivvy down in a sheltered spot
for the night. If you're lost on the mountain at night—
benighted—it is much the most sensible thing to do, so
long as you can keep warm. But the conditions at the
moment were so hazardous, and the lost walkers had little
experience or equipment. What sort of chance would they
stand?

They drove back in the Land-Rover to Cockermouth.
Dawn had become early morning. The fells were illuminated
by the first red-gold rays of the sun; the old town still shut
up in sleep. Wearily, they unloaded dogs and gear from the
back of the vehicle. The welcoming smell of food drifted
through the open door. Warm drinks . . .

'It looks as though this is turning into a big one. Can you
leave us Phil and Chris to search the gullies? We've got a
helicopter coming over anyway, so it's going to give us a
hand. We are getting increasingly worried about the snow
conditions . . .'

Chris was due back at work, so Phil was to be sent out
with the first party and another handler, to search the
gullies of Red Pike, where there was a particular risk of
avalanches. They were given dry clothes. Ropes and
equipment were reorganised, a stretcher and a cas bag for
each party. Shovels in case the two walkers had been
buried, and snow probes for avalanche searches. More
handlers to be deployed in the difficult areas where the
danger of avalanches was particularly acute . . .

A fresh, sunny morning, the great yellow aircraft
coming in with a huge noise, to land on the school field,
startling sleepy children to their windows, and housewives
hanging out a first load of washing. Handlers waiting for

the pilot's signal, then running in hunched up, with the dogs on leads. Tosh not at all keen, probably feeling she had done her bit. But she was held firmly by the waiting winchman, and immediately shot under the seat as soon as she was free to do so. Cockermouth fell away. The Buttermere fells were spread out in the glory of the morning, Ennerdale with its blue-shadowed lake breathtakingly beautiful, all tiredness vanished. Had he really been up all night?

The helicopter landed them and immediately took off. After the ear-shattering noise the silence was a tangible thing.

'Away, Tosh. Away . . .'

*   *   *

The two walkers who had given the alarm had spent an anxious night waiting, wondering what had happened to their friends, knowing that the search was going on but feeling helpless. So they were astonished and relieved when, shortly after dawn, their lost companions, very wet and very cold, staggered down the road towards the cottage. They were absolutely exhausted, having become lost and benighted, and having eventually scrambled down into Cleawes Gill and spent the night there. It had been a very long night indeed, huddled with a minimum of shelter—no bivvy sacs, no tent, no emergency survival gear—just in their clothes with rucksacks over their feet. Fortunately, the warm ground temperature, which had so increased the avalanche hazards on the mountainside, had probably saved their lives . . . they had been very, very lucky. But they were confused and cold, and in a fairly bad way nonetheless. When dawn had come, they had realised at last where they were and had used the last of their waning strength to get back onto the road and home to the cottage.

There was a phone box down the road. The first priority

must be to alert the police and through them the Mountain Rescue Team . . .

Jim Coyle was flying in the helicopter up towards Red Pike with the second party, when the police message came through to the pilot. The two lost walkers had turned up safe and well at the cottage in Loweswater. The search operation could be called off . . .

'Cockermouth Relay, do you read? Over.'

'Go ahead, Base.'

'Cockermouth Relay. Missing people have been located. I repeat, missing people have been located. Acknowledge. Over.'

'Cockermouth Base, message understood. People located.'

'Cockermouth Relay, inform all hill parties to return to Base.'

'Cockermouth One. Chopper will pick you up from Red Pike in zero five minutes . . .'

Phil made his way down once more to wait for the helicopter to pick him up and fly him down. There would be a cup of coffee, maybe, at Cockermouth Base, the usual debrief. If he was lucky he would get some more breakfast . . . and sleep. He suddenly remembered that today was the first day of the assessments. There wouldn't be any sleep after all. He was due up Langstrath that morning to assess the trainee dogs. Would the new dogs be able to cope with the kind of conditions the handlers had faced the night before? Would the dogs be able to function efficiently and do their job, however hazardous the terrain? That was what it was all about in the end. But it was going to be a long day!

11

A STRANGE INDICATION

A few weeks before Christmas 1988, John and Sam and I were asked to help organise and be involved in a documentary with BBC Radio Cumbria about Mountain Rescue and the work of the SARDA dogs, which was eventually broadcast in January 1989. A helicopter was being used for familiarisation training on a dog weekend, hosted by Cleveland SRT near Stokesley in North Yorkshire, and we had been given permission to fly with the crew.

We spent a wonderful day with the Cleveland team and SARDA dogs from all over the country, meeting up with old and new friends, and taking off and landing a number of times to get the newer dogs used to being moved about by helicopter. Sam behaved with his usual stoicism, only struggling to get into the helicopter as he always did at the last moment when he had had quite enough, thank you! Alison Colau's dog made a more positive statement— shooting as far under the seat as possible and staying there!

It was wonderful to fly over the North York moors, with the grouse skimming the heather beneath, and the glint of water in the narrow valleys, and a sense of space and freshness in the icy sunshine. In the evening there was the usual ceilidh, with guitars and singing, at the isolated Lion Inn on Blakey Rigg, right on top of the moor.

The next evening, I had a phone call from Graham Percival, the Cleveland dog handler who had organised the weekend. A quite extraordinary story began to emerge about events on the Sunday. I spent the whole evening making phone calls of my own . . .

Diane, one of the handlers, whose collie Patch is coming up to Novice this coming February on the Annual Course, had been working high up on an isolated part of the moor, far from any roads. It was a boggy area, thick with the deep heather, which always makes searching a difficult task. Patch had already found his first 'body', and was working well. Then, as the sun began to sink below the level of the moor and it grew cold, Patch, who was a few hundred yards away from his handler, quartering the ground for the second body, began to behave very oddly. Suddenly he almost screeched to a halt, ears up, tail up, a silly expression on his face. Diane thought for a moment, as he stood outlined against the evening sky, that he looked just like a cartoon Pluto. She was about to laugh when he began to back off very slowly, one foot at a time, his eyes fixed at a point on the ground.

'Oh God!' she thought. 'He's found a snake!'

Diane was not overfond of snakes, and this was undoubtedly adder country. She attempted to call him off, but still he stood with that mesmerised expression on his face.

'Away, Patch! Away, find!'

Whatever it was, it definitely wasn't the body! The signs were all wrong, and he was making no attempt to indicate.

'Away, Patch! Away, find!'

It was getting dark quickly now, and they were running out of time. She began to hurry through the heather towards him. This time he seemed to hear her and, recollecting his duty, began to move away up the moor, to begin searching again. But the mystery was too much for him, and once again he wheeled round and, galloping back to the spot in the heather, stood, tail up, ears up, staring fixedly at the ground.

A vague sense of dread overcame Diane as she scrambled somewhat breathlessly up to where the dog stood on a small promontory, his silhouette sharp in the sun's last brilliant burst of light. Despite its height, this was boggy ground, and she had to go carefully. At last she reached him. There were vivid green patches, and bog cotton grew in tufts here, deceptively safe looking.

'What on earth is it, Patch?'

He looked up at her, puzzled, relying on her to sort it out. She looked down, and a shock wave went through her. Half submerged in the tufts of vegetation, there lay what looked like a brownish sack, too light, maybe, to sink into the boggy ground which surrounded it. Very gingerly, she put one foot onto a clump of heather and leaned forward. Then she gave an exclamation of surprise.

'It's a dog, Patch. Would you believe it!'

Hardly a dog, though; no more really than a bag of bones, almost literally. But suddenly there was a movement from the tangle of limbs, a small sound from the emaciated ribcage. The dog whimpered. Patch, backing off again began to whine.

Diane, perched precariously now on two tussocks of grass, stood up and bellowed at the top of her voice, hoping that Mick Blood, her assessor, who was watching her through field glasses, would come and give a hand.

Then she bent down again.

'Hey!' She spoke softly. 'There's no need to be afraid.'

A hot dry tongue emerged from somewhere and rasped at her hand. She found herself swallowing hard.

'How long have you been up here, eh?'

Another twenty-four hours, and there wouldn't have been anything worth finding. She glanced up. There, above the prone body of the dog, the crows were wheeling round in the pink sky, round and round, waiting. Usually they didn't wait this long before they swooped down on a dying sheep, a young lamb, a horse with a broken leg, and pecked out its eyes.

'You're a very lucky dog. But how on earth did you get up here? There's not a footpath for miles, let alone a road . . . You're a real mystery . . .'

*   *   *

Two weeks before you might have seen a boxer dog called Chad, fighting fit and in superb condition, a splendid example of his breed, bouncing along through the heather. He was a much loved dog and he knew it. He had an owner and his wife who took him for wonderful walks, and three small boys who would give him a game whenever he wanted to play. The struggle for work in the depressed North-East was something many men had had to face, but it was a happy family and Chad's owner was especially glad of the beauty of the moors on the edge of the town. He and the dog could go for long walks together. It gave a purpose to the time spent waiting and hoping for work.

On this particular day Chad and his owner had been walking the path along the railway by Ingleby Bank. It was a clear sunny day. Perfect winter weather. Chad was in high spirits. There were unbelievable scents to investigate, streams to splash in, a vast tract of springy heather to run through. And then . . . the sight of a rabbit bouncing away, ears flat, through the auburn bracken. It was too much. Chad was a fast dog. He took off at top speed. The rabbit had a pretty good turn of speed, but maybe, just maybe, he was faster.

He could hear his master calling him, but it was only with half an ear. This was what he was born for—chasing rabbits. He could no longer see it, but the scent of the creatures was all around him, and one warm scent went on and on . . . down the bank, over the stream (there it was again!), through the small pine plantation, up the other side, until he fetched up against the small sandy hill where, somewhere in that pepperpot of holes, the creature had gone to ground.

Chad snuffled about for a while with his flat muzzle, hoping that one foolish rabbit might perhaps come out to play . . . but there was nothing doing. He was thirsty after the long run down the hill. He scrambled over the bank.

There at the bottom was a slow trickling stream, deep in
the peat, with a last patch of snow, left over from the
previous week's snowfall, gradually melting in the sun.
Chad had a good drink. Then he lifted his head and looked
around. His master had stopped calling, but it wouldn't
take him long to get back. He couldn't have come far, and
there would be a good scent once he was through the pines
. . . well, the wind was blowing at him from far, far away
down the valley side, but he was sure it wouldn't take him
long . . .

He began to trot back purposefully. Strange that his
master was no longer shouting for him. Perhaps after all he
had run farther than he thought. He trotted on. An hour
passed. Surely he hadn't been running that long. There
was confusing scents now. He no longer seemed to know
exactly where the wood began and ended. He was sure
that river had been on the far side of the bank. Now it was
here, somehow out of place. And it was bigger. Had it
grown bigger while he had been away?

He began to whine to himself, an empty space growing in
his insides which had only a little bit to do with hunger and
it almost being teatime. The light was fading rapidly over
the moor. It was growing colder. He must go faster if he
was to catch up with his master. He began to gallop
through the heather, his heart fixed on a place where he
knew his master must be . . . He ran on and on . . .

*   *   *

Chad's master was still looking for him, still shouting
himself hoarse, following the path he had seen Chad take,
then going up high where there was still light, scanning the
horizon. It was no good. Chad must have got himself
hopelessly lost. The moor suddenly seemed vast and
inhospitable, and incredibly lonely . . .

It was a hard thing to break to the children, that Chad
was lost. It was long after dark when he gave up looking,

and made his way home. That evening they phoned the local police stations and all the farmers in the area who were in the Yellow Pages, but to no avail. The next day they contacted all the local newspapers. Day after day, despite his own lack of transport, he made his way up to that point on the moor where Chad had last been seen. With all that publicity, surely someone somewhere had at least had a glimpse of a boxer dog. Could it possibly be that he was still there, up on the moor, running frantically, seeking his master?

The previous week there had been a cold snap and heavy snowfalls had transformed the moor into a wonderland of beauty, but lethal to any creature unused to its harshness. Now the weather, thankfully, seemed set fair for a bit; most of the snow had gone, but the nights were still bitter, and there were wet days, days when the rain hurled against the windows at night, and they all thought to themselves that, somewhere out there, Chad might still be alive—wet, cold, hungry, and frightened. It was almost too much to bear.

But as the days passed, and there was no sign, no sighting, nothing . . . they began to try to come to terms with the idea that no dog, short of some miracle, could possibly have survived that long . . .

*   *   *

Mick Blood and the other handlers who had been nearby came running towards Diane through the heather. The dog began to struggle, trying to get to its feet, half-sinking into the soft ground. She could see now that it was a boxer, a lovely creature once. But were they in time, or was it already too late?

'Lie still! We'll take care of you.'

It must be desperate for food. There was moisture in the ground, a brackish pool just within reach. Was that how it had stayed alive when it was too weak to move about any more? The weather had been unseasonably mild, otherwise it wouldn't have had a chance, and if Patch hadn't alerted them, what were the chances, ever, of anyone else passing this way . . . ?

Mick Blood had caught up with them, as surprised as she was by the find. They rooted in Diane's sack, looking for something warm to wrap the dog in. The next hour or so could be crucial.

Gently they carried him the long distance over the moor to the last point where the Land-Rover had been able to get up the narrow track. He was wrapped now in warm jumpers gleaned from several sacks. Patch trotted behind, looking proprietorial and proud of himself. The boxer was obviously exhausted but nonetheless spent precious energy trying to lick everyone within reach. Most of the food had been eaten up during the course of the day, but a warm cup-a-soup poured into an empty sandwich box was greeted with almost hysterical hunger. Then it was full speed to the nearest vet.

'Well, I can't find too much wrong with him, you'll be relieved to know. He's strained his back legs. He must have run and run until his legs gave out. But time and rest and good feeding should do the trick. He's an extremely lucky dog!'

They breathed a sigh of relief. It was time to try the police station to see if they could find an owner, who by now must surely have given up hope!

*   *   *

It was obvious now that Chad was never coming home.

The children had been heartbroken. The house, usually so full of Chad's exuberance, seemed very empty. At last, with a heavy heart, the decision was taken to try to give a home to a dog from the Boxer Rescue . . .

They had reckoned without the phone call. Yet how could it be possible, after all this time? It had to be a mistake. The Land-Rover drew up outside the house. They could see, through the window a dog being lifted out. For a moment they were sure it wasn't Chad after all. So small and thin—for a moment the thought came to Chad's owner that it was a cocker spaniel, that they had made a terrible mistake. How would they ever explain to the children . . . ? Then they opened the door and suddenly they knew it was all right after all. The pathetic bundle, still swathed in odd jumpers, was brought into the hall.

Chad looked up at his master. They laid him on the floor. He seemed too weak to stand. Then suddenly, out of the corner of his eye, Chad caught sight of an intruder. Another dog had come to usurp his place—the dog from the Boxer Rescue, who had only just arrived. Suddenly he was on his feet, scattering sweaters everywhere. He wasn't having any of that! This was his home, and he would make sure everyone knew it!

'I think he's going to be all right!' The team leader grinned at Chad. 'But there might be other problems you hadn't counted on!'

The dog from the Boxer Rescue had to be found a good home on a nearby farm, with a family who had been waiting and hoping for a dog. And Chad was back where he belonged, enjoying a great deal of attention and a lot of spoiling.

And it was all thanks to a rather unusual find by a SARDA dog, which might or might not get into the record books . . . it was all part of the job . . .

12

BIVVY DOWN BROWN

'There's no way I would go up there, all alone, knowing there might be a body up there, if I didn't have the dog for company . . . he looks after me, and I look after him.' Experienced SARDA handler.

'A couple of hours later finds three of us and our dogs searching a footpath, not ideal deployment. I branch off to increase the search area and eventually come out onto the ridge, only to be enveloped by clag which necessitates some consideration of which way I should be going. By the time I rejoin the others, Sam is weakening fast. There was a time when to work for hours at a time was no problem, but not any more. Never mind, in an hour or so it will be light. There's only one thing for it. The gortex bivvy sacs given to us by a local firm based in Appleby will prove very useful now . . .' John Brown.

It has been a long, long night. Snow and ice on the tops, lethally dangerous once you feel yourself go, ankles aching with the effort of kick-kicking to gain a toehold with crampons on the steep-sided crag, Sam crabbing his way across the ridge, his claws scrabbling for pawholds; it doesn't do to think that below you the snowfield falls steeply for seven hundred feet.

It is an eerie place at night, and somewhere out there in the vast night of the mountain, a body may be lying, maybe at the base of the crag, having slipped and fallen. But now a freezing mist creates shapes in the hollows of the fell, whipped up by the thin wind which comes and goes, moaning to itself, emphasising the desolation.

Dear Sam. He gets tired now so quickly, but he goes on and on, trying, until it is up to John to say . . . 'Stop.' He is a warm, infinitely comforting presence in a world which has been here since before humanity began and will still be here afterwards. It remains and we come and go. It is because of a sense of this wildness that men have built cities and filled them with lights and central heating and double glazing, to keep out the loneliness. And it is on nights like this, when the wildness is all about you, that you remember why.

But perversely, it is this very wildness that so many seek to find again. It is like a hunger, to climb and climb until the noise of civilisation, with its stresses and its jaded life, is forgotten for a little while, and the things of the spirit return.

But it is dangerous. It has to be, because that is the nature of wild places. And people fall up here and sometimes they are killed. However well-prepared they might be, things go wrong. There is no safety net to catch the unwary or the unlucky. That is the choice you make.

People say, if I were in a Mountain Rescue Team, or had a Search Dog, I'd get furious, having to go out, risk my own life, team members' lives, because other people make fools of themselves on the mountains. And there are some stupid people about, you can't deny that. But team members feel it isn't up to the MRT to make judgements. They are there to help. They know all about what draws people into the fells, because a love of these wild places is in them, too. They understand how it is. And one day, when they are climbing in the Alps or Scotland or Spain, or maybe even in their own fells, at their own back door, another team might do the same for them . . .

This man they are all looking for, you couldn't say he had done anything wrong. He had all the proper gear, and a map in a plastic sleeve, and good boots and wet weather clothing and a warm drink and food, and an ice axe and crampons—all the essentials for winter hill-walking. He was getting on a bit, but he was pretty fit, and he didn't want anyone to wrap him up in cotton wool. A Wainwright man, you could say, who followed the master guide-maker and knew every cleft and valley in the Lakes and loved them all.

But now he is lost out here, in this inhospitable terrain, with the temperature fifteen degrees below—more with the wind-chill factor. And above the black waters of the lake, six Search Dogs are patiently quartering the ground, hoping to find him before it's too late . . .

Dear Sam. For John he is the very best companion of all, to wander the dark. And perhaps Sam feels the same way about John. For years now they have given each other faithful service, and who knows where one half of the team begins and the other ends? It is a total partnership. They understand one another.

Now Sam is reading his master's head, the way he does, and he knows it is important to search that great empty black space he can sense stretching out over the snowfield below the ridge. He can feel the free wind in his nose, he knows the way the ground lies. The air flows past him, telling him things we can't imagine. John sends him away, but he knows already what to do.

They search on and on, taking out slices of the high ground. They gain the upper stretches of the ridge. The wind blasts at them here, and Sam moves crabwise to keep his balance. Could the walker have fallen from here after all? Suddenly a gibbous moon appears over the fells, chased by ragged snow clouds all across the peak. The world seems to turn under the sky, the moving clouds giving the appearance that everything, even the great fell, is racing past, spinning forever round the shining lake below. Snow blasts at them, blinding John. He digs in with his ice axe until the brief storm is past.

Sam comes back. Old now, he shudders and lopes. His

nose, pig rootling, asks for comfort. John and Sam can give something to each other after all. Sam is part of the mountain. He has the animal understanding of it, of its very skin, which he feels with his broken paws; of its breath, which he breathes; of its voice, which he hears when John hears nothing but the 'squelch' of the radio. John is relying on Sam to tell him about the night. There is total trust between them.

But Sam is tired, snuffling with his nose in the snow, playing a little. The cloud comes down out of the sky, enveloping them suddenly and unpredictably in a freezing mist. There seems no way forward. The torchlight bounces back.

They have covered their area and John knows it is time to stop for a rest. They have been searching now for hours, since the call came from team headquarters for all available SARDA dogs. He presses the radio button, but the Land-Rover in the valley is behind a crag and there is only the 'squelch' for company. Sam can't keep going all night the way he used to, and for both of them a couple of hours' kip on the fellside means that he doesn't have to come all the long, weary way down to start again at first light. Gaining height gets harder for an old dog, and once you are there, it makes sense to stay . . .

The mist has cleared again, and the lake shines out under a clear moon, unimaginable silver. It is one of those moments that men and women would sell their souls for, and certainly risk their lives. A silent, breathless, windless moment with the snowfield falling away from the ridge and the ridge itself black against a dark blue sky, and stars cut out like diamond chips and the whole vastness of the Milky Way flung like a scarf above it all. Certain things, in these moments, are understood, and never quite forgotten. But then the wind bites again, a punishment perhaps for foolish godlike thoughts, an icy cloud of snow crystals permeating everything.

They lose a little ground, climbing down towards the

lake. There is a small plateau here, under the lee of the ridge. John makes a low retaining wall with the snow. Sam roots with his nose, contributing nothing. John searches with his torch for the bivvy sack. He puts on all the spare clothing he is carrying with him; the end of the rucksack will go over his feet. He opens the hooped end of the bivvy sack and crawls in. Sam, eager to be out of the cold, scrabbles in alongside, a gangle of snowy paws everywhere. There is a brief argument between them, soon forgotten. Sam smells of wet and old fur. But he is warm to be beside and an infinite comfort. Almost immediately he begins to snore immoderately, more exhausted than he will admit.

John is very tired, too, but strangely wakeful, glad only to be warm. Without waking Sam he attempts to get at his sandwiches but gives up. The snow rattles on the outside of the tent. On the other side of the water there is a long, winding road. All evening at the wonderful hotel halfway down the lake, the one with the stunning views and the balcony like something out of a Noel Coward play, someone has been celebrating a 21st birthday party. Fairy lights are reflected intermittently in the face of the lake. Now headlights sweep past, on their way home again, lighting up the secret face of the mountain as they pass, unaware that farther down the side of the lake a Land-Rover waits with a patient cold Controller hunched over the radio. The staff of the hotel know. They have helped out before on rescues. Their hotel is marked on the Ordnance Survey map as a Mountain Rescue Post. It is the only building in the valley, and later, perhaps, they will provide hot food and succour to the searchers while they wait for reinforcements. But just now no one wants to spoil the party . . . not for a little while.

In the first dawn light Sam and John will wake, cold now and stiff, and work their way down to a new search area. And a little later still, a handler and her dog in another part of the range, up behind the hotel, will come upon the stiffening body of the walker who had died instantly after a fall of some 600 feet down the snowfield the previous day. A helicopter, brought in to help with the search at first light, will winch the body from a high, almost inaccessible point far above the lake.

But for the moment the dawn is a little way off. The fairy lights go out one by one at the hotel, and the headlamps sweep home along the drystone wall, and Sam sleeps. His bones ache, and he is tired. He and John have seen life and death together. Now it is almost time to hang up the red jacket, for honourable retirement, for a rest from the hill. Almost time to say goodbye to the midnight phone call, and the excitement of the night search, of that wonderful blood-stirring call—AWAY, SAM, AWAY, FIND!'

Sam remembers. His paws twitch and he dreams . . .

13

LOCKERBIE

'If anything is to be learned from this dreadful tragedy of "man's inhumanity to man", then it must be that of trust evolved over the long days of working together. For me it was a great privilege to have worked with so many people who gave of their time. No one could have asked for better.'
Search Co-ordinator, Kielder.

It was early evening on Wednesday, 21st December, 1988. Bill Parr, Southern Scotland's SARDA co-ordinator and a member of the Moffat Hill Rescue Team, was feeding his dogs outside the back door of his home in Lockerbie when there was an earth-shattering bang. A few moments later the whole sky lit up as a huge fireball mounted above the small town. Night was transformed for long seconds into a harsh, unforgiving daylight.

Bill's first thought was that he was witnessing a nuclear explosion, and those were the feelings of many other residents that night as they stood transfixed, outside their doors, watching the terrible blazing sky. But for others, there had been no time to think or feel anything. For the 259 passengers and crew of the Boeing 747 Jumbo Pan-Am Flight PA103, for some of the residents of Sherwood Crescent, and for a number of motorists who had been driving along the A74 at the precise moment when the jumbo jet fell out of the sky, death had come without warning.

Bill tried for long minutes to contact the police, unable to do so at first as all the lines were jammed. No one as yet had any clear idea of what might have happened. It hadn't been so long since two fast jets had collided just south of the Border near the small town of Appleby. Had it happened again? It seemed a more likely explanation. Eventually he managed to get through, to be requested to go down to the police station immediately with his dog . . .

He was on his way to join the police dog teams when a frightened woman ran up to him in the darkness, asking for help. She told Bill that there was wreckage in the field alongside the church—possibly two aircraft, and could he please come and give a hand. It was an awful night, high wind and stormy, and now that the unearthly glow had almost faded from the sky, to be replaced by a strange orange light in the distance, it was hard to see. But they found the field at last and Bill shone his torch. What he saw was the nose cone of the Boeing, and in those few dreadful seconds, as the beam of light picked out the debris in the field, the horror of what had happened became clear . . .

By just after midnight there were twenty-one Search Dog teams working in the area of Lockerbie, having been urgently summoned by Bill's wife Mona. Some had travelled as far as 150 miles from their homes. Bill and his dog had gone out immediately with two police dog teams. The main impact area, Sherwood Crescent, where the body of the aircraft had come down, was still on fire. The streets were littered with glass and rubble. Firemen were working flat out, damping down burning buildings. But it was a very haphazard undertaking: the whole area reeked of aviation fuel. It was pitch black and the weather was dreadful. And no one even knew if there would be any survivors at all . . . One of the first rescuers on the scene expressed his feelings on arriving at the main site of the crashed 747:

'We rigged up the lights and switched them on. But it was such a terrible sight that our instinct was to switch them off again immediately, so we would not have to face what was there, in front of us . . .

SARDA handlers were employed, from that first night, out in the fields, around the town, where so many pieces of wreckage, and so many of the bodies, were strewn; and in the smouldering ruins of buildings, the ground saturated with aircraft fuel to such an extent that dogs and men were to become ill in the ensuing days from continuous exposure to the fumes, and in the case of the dogs, from contact with skin and coats. Later it would become necessary to restrict the dogs and handlers to three seven-hour days within the impact zone, working for spells of twenty minutes and resting for fifteen . . .

Very quickly, dogs from Ireland, other areas of Scotland and the whole of England and Wales were called to the search, and were involved in the harrowing task of locating bodies, wreckage from the aircraft, and personal effects. It was a search which went on all over Christmas, with only one day's break for Christmas Day, exacting its own toll on families, too. It involved, in the Lockerbie area alone, 48 different dog teams, peaking with 40 dog teams on one single day (Boxing Day) and the search covered 100 national grid squares, the area around the town where the aircraft wreckage was strewn in a long trail of dreadful destruction.

As the first night drew on, the full horror of what they were faced with become apparent. As the Flight Commander from 'A' Flight, RAF Boulmer expressed it, after flying across the search area, seeing the crashed aircraft for the first time picked out in the helicopter searchlights:

'I'll never forget seeing the long line of pieces of fuselage, emergency chutes and bodies stretching for miles over the countryside . . .'

It was to take an enormous emotional and physical toll on all who were involved . . . 'the biggest major incident, turning into the biggest murder hunt this country has ever known', as the Kielder Search Co-ordinator said when at last the search, after long days stretching into the New Year, began to draw to a close. It was to bring rescuers and searchers together in an extraordinary bond of mutual support, a recognition of something shared, of a community and individuals sharing suffering and help. The workers at the Academy in Lockerbie (the co-ordination centre for the town)—the WRVS, the school meals service, the 'unsung heroines' who somehow, miraculously, organised a school meals service to feed hundreds of rescue workers twenty-four hours a day, within hours of the disaster; the Salvation Army who day and night were out on the streets offering hot drinks, food and comfort; the Samaritans—supporting bereaved and rescuers alike; the RAF Search and Rescue Sea King, and the Wessex helicopters, the Pumas, the Chinook and the Squirrel which were on constant stand-by; the Ambulance Service, the Fire Service, Mountain Rescue teams, the Police who moved so fast to get it all together . . .

The work of SARDA has been highly praised, as has that of all the rescue services, and their contribution was considered to be outstanding. Many handlers freely con-fessed to having at some stage given way to tears. For men and women used even to the most traumatic work of mountain rescue this was to prove a stern and terrible test. In the burned out remains of houses, sifting through the charred rubble in roofless shells of what had so recently been homes preparing for Christmas, confronting the sadness of sudden death, whether in the air or on the ground, was to face stark tragedy on a scale unprecedented in their already wide experience. Even for Dave Riley, who had memories of El Salvador behind him, and years of seeing the worst that human beings could do to one another as a policeman on the beat. For them all, it was something they would never forget.

In the last stages of the search I went over into Northumberland to see the work of some of the searchers, who were by then looking for sections of wreckage and personal effects which might help in identification of the air crash victims. It was slow, painstaking and saddening work. The search involved members of Northumberland National Park Fell Rescue Team, SARDA handlers and SARDA dogs, members of the North East Search Panel, the Yorkshire Dales and Peak District teams, as well as many other volunteers, with Brian Wright of the Cleveland team as Co-ordinator, working with Northumbria Police in a unique co-operation. They had been searching since 23rd December for parts of the tail section. This was now early January.

I was the guest of Northumbria Police Force, who were in overall charge of the massive search operation. Wreckage of the plane stretched from coast to coast across Northern England in two trails of devastation, aided by the high winds. Tail sections of the Boeing 747 had fallen on Kielder Forest, the biggest man-made forest in Europe, and over the area of the Kielder Dam, the deepest man-made lake. The total search area in Northumberland covered by the Police Authority was 170 square miles of some of the wildest, most inhospitable countryside in Britain, and such dense forest, amounting to 110 square miles of the total area, that no searchers, not even dogs, could penetrate most of it.

This was gruelling work, the dogs and the line searchers combing the rides which cut through the conifers at intervals, and where they could, fighting their way into the almost windless darkness under the trees. I had seen the maps at the Control Centre—the small police station in the picturesque village of Bellingham which had suddenly become Incident HQ for Kielder, along with the local school, where up to 250 men and women had been given sleeping space on hall floors and in classrooms for the duration of the search. I had seen the areas which had been so meticulously coloured and blocked in, day by day.

To see it 'on the ground', with the attendant problems, was to realise that a tremendous job was being done, here as in all the search areas, with total dedication, hour after hour, day after day. Under the conifers, which had been growing unthinned since just after the Second World War, there was an eerie half-light. Branches snatched and clung. Paths suddenly disappeared, and perspectives altered. It would be so easy to get lost. All handlers had to have a navigator with them for just such a reason. And morale, too, was important. It was perhaps better not to search alone. As we drove up the rides into the Forest, axle deep in mud, I could see, after all this time, sections of fuselage below us on the treetops, cradled by the topmost branches of the dark firs: inaccessible, even by helicopter.

Perhaps the whole tremendous effort in Kielder is best summed up by the words of the team leader of Northumberland National Park Fell Rescue Team, the host team, who found such a willing response from so many volunteers all eager to do something to help—218 of them on the last memorable weekend:

> I was lost for words at the response from MR teams on the weekend of 7th to 8th January. Such an event had never been seen before. The camaraderie and sense of purpose was unequalled and had to be seen to be believed. Due to this response, MR teams have gained much credibility with the Police . . . I was proud to be part of it.

*   *   *

It had been raining in Lockerbie the day I went. We drove along the A74 and there, suddenly, shockingly, we were faced with the full horror of the aftermath. We had kept away, not wanting to get in the way when we couldn't help, in a place which already had too many press, too many cameras, prying into private grief. Somehow, we expected that now there would be nothing . . . But there it was, by the side of the road: the blackened stumps of buildings, like a war, a great hole in the ground with nothing, no sign of what had once been there, like pictures I had seen of a

village, somewhere, anywhere, after a mortar bombard-
ment . . .

We drove on, not speaking—too shocked to speak—into
the little town square which had become so familiar from
the television screen. Flowers were massed in one corner
by the Academy building. I remembered the beautiful scarf I
had seen brought in after the day's search at Kielder, the
colours so bright and glowing . . . I remembered the couple
who had come out one night from their home and told the
Search Dog handlers how comforting it was for them,
when they were too afraid to sleep, to know that the dogs
and men were working close by. They had given biscuits to
the dogs . . . I remembered the WRVS ladies who had given
comfort and succour day after day to the weary searchers,
even when they themselves had been victims of terrible
loss . . . I remembered the children who had died, in the
town and in the air, the thought of whom had made it all so
doubly heartbreaking, and for some, so terrible that for a
while they were unable to go on. But above all I
remembered the caring and the courage of townspeople
and rescuers and the great outpouring of love felt by
everyone who had been there. I remembered the words of
one of my friends, a dog handler, who had been so moved
by the kindness and the love and the gratitude of the people
on the ground, that he found his own return home to his
family at Christmastime almost unbearable after what he
had seen . . .

'How could we complain of being tired and hungry and
even distressed by all that we were experiencing? These
people, in a few seconds, had lost everything. We could do
nothing but bring comfort to relatives by searching for the
bodies of their loved ones . . . nothing we could do would
ever be enough . . .'

The feelings of all those rescuers and the people of
Lockerbie, and of people everywhere, were symbolised in
the bouquets and wreaths of flowers before me, heaped on
the pavement, still fresh in the rain. There were wreaths

there from the American People, from people in the town, from searchers and workers in the Rescue Services, from the Search and Rescue Dog Association itself. I laid my own small bunch of flowers for them all.

EPILOGUE

We had only known for three weeks, but despite a visit to Liverpool Veterinary Hospital there was nothing to be done. Sam had bone cancer, and it was advancing fast. The next day, the day before Christmas Eve, as the other SARDA dogs searched the ground at Lockerbie for survivors of the plane crash, the Browns' local vet came to the house. John had taken Sam for a last walk. They had, in John's words, 'had a chat', and now in his own familiar kitchen, in his own place, he was put to sleep.

He had been on the call-out list until almost the very end, and he had never until now had to be left behind when the phone had rung in the kitchen, which we had feared he would hate so much. But it was very hard to say goodbye. It had been a good life, and a useful one. He had exhausted more than his nine lives in his rumbustuous rough-and-tumble years. And he was loved so much as a special family dog, and by so many other friends . . .

In the context of the horrendous tragedy of Lockerbie it seems almost foolish to grieve for one old dog, who had almost had his day. But we loved him, all of us, for his madcap ways, for his bravery and his great heart. He brought us charm and laughter and warmth in what is sometimes a cold world. There is room for many kinds of love and many kinds of grief. And we have shed tears too for Sam, and felt his loss, and we will never forget him.

For me, he will always have a special place in my heart.